Survival Kit

THE AZRIELI SERIES OF HOLOCAUST SURVIVOR MEMOIRS: PREVIOUSLY PUBLISHED TITLES

Survival Kit

Zuzana Sermer

THE AZRIELI FOUNDATION
www.azrielifoundation.org

Cover and book design by Mark Goldstein
Endpaper maps by Martin Gilbert
Map on page xxvii by François Blanc

LIBRARY AND ARCHIVES CANADA CATALOGUING IN PUBLICATION

Sermer, Zuzana
     Survival kit/ Zuzana Sermer.

(The Azrieli series of Holocaust survivor memoirs. Series v)
Includes bibliographical references and index.
ISBN 978-1-897470-32-9

1. Sermer, Zuzana. 2. Holocaust, Jewish (1939–1945) – Slovakia – Personal narratives. 3. Holocaust survivors – Canada – Biography. I. Azrieli Foundation II. Title. III. Series: Azrieli series of Holocaust survivor memoirs. Series v

D804.196.S46 2012   940.53'18092   C2012-905453-4

PRINTED IN CANADA

The Azrieli Series of Holocaust Survivor Memoirs

Contents

Series Preface:
In their own words...

In telling these stories, the writers have liberated themselves. For so many years we did not speak about it, even when we became free people living in a free society. Now, when at last we are writing about what happened to us in this dark period of history, knowing that our stories will be read and live on, it is possible for us to feel truly free. These unique historical documents put a face on what was lost, and allow readers to grasp the enormity of what happened to six million Jews – one story at a time.

David J. Azrieli, C.M., C.Q., M.Arch
Holocaust survivor and founder, The Azrieli Foundation

Since the end of World War II, over 30,000 Jewish Holocaust survivors have immigrated to Canada. Who they are, where they came from, what they experienced and how they built new lives for themselves and their families are important parts of our Canadian heritage. The Azrieli Foundation's Holocaust Survivor Memoirs Program was established to preserve and share the memoirs written by those who survived the twentieth-century Nazi genocide of the Jews of Europe and later made their way to Canada. The program is guided by the conviction that each survivor of the Holocaust has a remarkable story to tell, and that such stories play an important role in education about tolerance and diversity.

Millions of individual stories are lost to us forever. By preserving the stories written by survivors and making them widely available to a broad audience, the Azrieli Foundation's Holocaust Survivor Memoirs Program seeks to sustain the memory of all those who perished at the hands of hatred, abetted by indifference and apathy. The personal accounts of those who survived against all odds are as different as the people who wrote them, but all demonstrate the courage, strength, wit and luck that it took to prevail and survive in such terrible adversity. The memoirs are also moving tributes to people – strangers and friends – who risked their lives to help others, and who, through acts of kindness and decency in the darkest of moments, frequently helped the persecuted maintain faith in humanity and courage to endure. These accounts offer inspiration to all, as does the survivors' desire to share their experiences so that new generations can learn from them.

The Holocaust Survivor Memoirs Program collects, archives and publishes these distinctive records and the print editions are available free of charge to libraries, educational institutions and Holocaust-education programs across Canada, and at Azrieli Foundation educational events. They are also available for sale to the general public at bookstores. All editions of the books are available for free download on our web site at: www.azrielifoundation.org.

The Azrieli Foundation would like to express appreciation to the following people for their invaluable efforts in producing this series: Sherry Dodson (Maracle Press), Sir Martin Gilbert, Stan Greenspan, Mia Spiro, Keaton Taylor, Sylvia Vance, and Margie Wolfe and Emma Rodgers of Second Story Press.

About the Glossary

The following memoir contains a number of terms, concepts and historical references that may be unfamiliar to the reader. For information on major organizations; significant historical events and people; geographical locations; religious and cultural terms; and foreign-language words and expressions that will help give context and background to the events described in the text, please see the glossary beginning on page 119.

Introduction

Zuzana Sermer (née Weinberger) begins her memoir of surviving World War II with an unanswerable question: "How can I explain the unexplainable?" In voicing this, she echoes the queries that every Holocaust survivor must have asked himself or herself: Why did I survive when so many perished? Was it by fate or chance, quick thinking or luck? Sermer's memoir, *Survival Kit*, is an elaboration of her answer, formulated long after the events. In the end, she comes to the conclusion that her own survival is the result of "luck, coincidence and occurrences that I have come to think of as miracles."

Survival Kit is at once a history of the German invasion of Czechoslovakia and Hungary and a meditation on the vagaries of chance and the naive bravery that allowed her to escape time and time again from the clutches of a seemingly inevitable fate. Sermer credits her husband, Arthur, with the strength and boldness that rescued them from hopelessness again and again. Theirs is a love story and one of lasting togetherness that moves from Czechoslovakia to German-occupied Slovakia to Hungary and back again, this time to Communist Czechoslovakia, and finally to Canada. Their revenge for those they lost was to stay alive, live well and create new generations. Zuzana and Arthur, who passed away in 2003, had four children and eight grandchildren; they established themselves in Toronto in 1968, where Zuzana still lives.

Sermer began to write after the war, while raising her children in Slovakia. A keen observer of political and family life, her articles appeared in magazines and newspapers. There was often a moral to her stories, but the story she tells here is not so certain. It is, rather, a story searching for a moral. It's a story of good fortune, when Holocaust stories generally contain so little, and what Sermer calls her "miracles": "My parents' love, my bold naïveté, the courage and determination of my fiancé." Sermer is the lucky and plucky heroine in a story that turns out well. To the question of whether we need another story of the Holocaust at all, Sermer replies, "The conclusion I have reached is that these are our stories to tell, and tell them we should. It is up to others to decide if they will read them—my hope is that they will."

In her memoir, Zuzana Sermer introduces us to Humenné, the town at the foot of the Carpathian Mountains in Czechoslovakia where she was born on August 29, 1924. Czechoslovakia was established as a country in the aftermath of World War I, when the 1921 Treaty of Trianon dissolved the Austro-Hungarian Empire. The treaty left Hungary with a third of its territories and population although the countries that were split off from Hungary – the current-day Romania, Slovakia, Serbia, Ukraine, Croatia, Austria and Slovenia – had large numbers of ethnic Hungarians and Hungarian speakers. A quarter of the Slovak population who considered themselves Hungarian in language and in culture suddenly found themselves minorities in a foreign country. But they assimilated quickly. Even though her family spoke Hungarian at home, Sermer grew up loving her nation of Czechoslovakia, "a pearl of democracy" under the leadership of Tomáš Masaryk, the nation's "father." Jews made up approximately 135,000 of the four million Slovak population and the idyll Sermer describes was not uncommon: mixed Jewish and Christian neighbourhoods and friendships, a good education in Slovak, Czech and Hungarian, a tolerant nation, a pious and humble father and a loving family. Sermer attended secular school and, on Sunday, the

Beth Jacob school for girls run by the very Orthodox Agudah, an organization holding that nothing worldly should come between Jews and the study of the Torah. In contrast, the religious and Zionist Mizrachi movement, which taught that the Torah and "working the Land of Israel went hand in hand," appealed to many in Sermer's hometown. Zuzana joined the Mizrachi youth group Bnei Akiva, but writes that she was most affected by her parents' values.

All that changed with the German occupation of Czechoslovakia (1938–1945), which began with the Munich Agreement of September 29–30, 1938. Without the consultation of Czechoslovakia, the major European powers sought to appease Germany by allowing the Nazis to annex Czechoslovakia's northern and western border regions of Bohemia, Moravia and Silesia, known collectively as the Sudetenland. Ostensibly, the rationale for this was to alleviate the suffering of ethnic Germans in the regions that had been granted to Czechoslovakia twenty-one years earlier. On March 16, 1939, however, the German Wehrmacht moved into the remainder of Czechoslovakia and, from Prague Castle, Hitler proclaimed Czechoslovakia to be reconstituted as the Protectorate of Bohemia and Moravia and the independent state of Slovakia. Despite its nominal independence, however, Slovakia was controlled by and allied with Nazi Germany. Hitler further gave Hungary, as beneficiaries of the Munich accord, the green light to invade its lost territories and the Hungarian army marched into Slovakia, quickly occupying the Subcarpathia up to the border with Poland as part of the nation's dream to reassemble the greater Hungary.

Sermer's personal ordeal begins in 1935 with her mother's illness, though she is well aware that something was "festering" all over Europe. The fall of the Spanish Republic to Franco's Fascists in March 1939 was a turning point, and one that coincided with the invasion of Czechoslovakia. Hitler installed a puppet government, Hlinka's Slovak People's Party, a fascist, antisemitic and Catholic nationalist group that had been established during the Austro-Hungarian

Empire and reconstituted in 1925. It quickly established an authoritarian stance and began to harass both leftist and Jewish political parties, manipulating the electoral process to obtain more than 97 per cent of the vote in the Slovak general election of December 1938. The loyalty of Slovak Jews to the new independent nation was questioned, particularly given that many of them identified with Hungary and Hungarian culture.

The Hlinka Party, led by Father Jozef Tiso, passed its first anti-Jewish law in Slovakia on April 18, 1939. Jews were expelled from all government positions and service and, by the fall, the military. Jewish children were barred from attending school, but fifteen-year-old Sermer was already out of school, was unable to afford the cost, and was needed at home to look after her ailing mother.

In August 1940, Eichmann sent his representative SS-Haupsturm-führer Dieter Wisliceny to Bratislava as an adviser on Jewish affairs. The Hlinka Guard, the paramilitary wing of the Hlinka Slovak People's Party established in October 1938, and the Slovak volunteers in the SS, the Freiwillige Schutzstaffel, willingly helped Hitler carry out his plans and became the well-armed fist used to enforce the restrictions against the Jews.

The anti-Jewish restrictions intensified and by the fall of 1940 Jews were no longer allowed to go to the market, own a radio or keep property or valuable assets. Sermer and her friends gravitated to Hashomer Hatzair (The Youth Guard), a Socialist-Zionist youth movement that promoted immigration to the British mandate of Palestine. Some members managed to leave just in time – by 1940, more than 6,000 Jews had emigrated, both legally and illegally. Shortly after Germany's invasion of the Soviet Union on June 22, 1941, Slovakia entered World War II as an ally of Germany. In September 1941, the Slovak government passed the "Jewish Code," anti-Jewish legislation modelled on the Nuremberg Laws that redefined Jews as a racial rather than a religious or national group and required them to be identified by yellow armbands and cloth Stars of David. As Sermer observes, social differences that once divided Jews according to class began to dissolve in the face of a threat that lumped them together under one imposed category.

Slovakia was the first Axis partner to embrace the "Final Solution" and enthusiastically made plans for the deportation of its approximately 89,000 remaining Jews. Humenné and its vicinity were among the places in which the deportations began. The first transport, which focused on single women being taken for forced labour, was scheduled for March 25, 1942, and Sermer decided that as an only child who was needed at home, she had to find a way to avoid the deportation. She begged the Slovakian police to allow her to stay and look after her mother and, when the quota was met, she was allowed to return home. That initial transport of single women went straight to Auschwitz and the women from Humenné, including Sermer's friend Eva, became some of the early Jewish inmates in the camp. This was the first of Sermer's miraculous escapes. Between March and October 1942, fifty-seven transports carrying close to 59,000 Jewish deportees left Slovakia. Thirty-eight trains with nearly 40,000 Jews went to the Lublin district in Poland; the other nineteen transports, with 18,600 people, were taken to Auschwitz.

Following that first transport, Sermer went into hiding, moving between attics, cellars and crawlspaces, harboured by Catholic neighbours even in the face of grave personal danger. Only about 19,000 Jews – most of whom had certificates of exemption on the grounds that they were essential to the country's economy – remained in Slovakia. Being poor, Sermer's family had nothing with which to negotiate so her father obtained a certificate of conversion to the Greek Orthodox Church, issued by a priest who felt more hatred for the Catholic Hlinka than the dwindling Jews. The certificate would not save her father in the end, but it provided a rationale for Sermer to beg for his safety when he was arrested at a synagogue with other men determined to form a minyan, the quorum of Jewish men required for certain prayers, his certificate of conversion in his pocket. Sermer's account points to the lack of logic in both compliance and defiance, where neither is the predictor of survival. Sermer is candid about the horrifying decisions her family made for self-protection, describing a scene in which her father turned away her aunt and her cousins in order to protect his wife and his daughter. There was simply no space to hide anyone in their single room; nevertheless, the decision still haunts Sermer, as do dreams of her small cousin Erwin who did not survive.

With the death of her mother in July 1943 and her father now interned among the 3,500 Jews held in the forced labour camps in Nováky, Vyhne, Sered' and Ilava – the latter reserved for people with certificates of conversion – Sermer decided to escape to Hungary. She had recently met Arthur Sermer, the man who would become her husband, his brother Victor and their cousin Leah, all three of whom had hidden in the forest to escape deportation. They were among the nearly 10,000 Jews who fled to Hungary in hopes of sanctuary even though President Tiso had stopped the deportations from Slovakia as a result of reports, in part through the Papal Nuncio in Bratislava, that the Germans were murdering the deported Jews in German-occupied Poland. Tiso hesitated and then refused to deport the remaining 24,000 Jews in Slovakia in the autumn of 1942. Nonetheless, Slovak Jews like Sermer were afraid that their reprieve was only temporary.

In January 1944, at the age of nineteen, Zuzana, Arthur, Victor and Leah were smuggled across the border by horse carriage to the relative safety of Hungary. Like Slovakia, the country was ambivalent about its relationship to Germany and to its Jewish citizens. Hungary had enacted one of the first anti-Jewish laws in Europe in 1920 and was quick to sign on to the German "Final Solution," but there had been strong opposition. On May 28, 1938, both houses of parliament, widely supported in the upper house by representatives of the Catholic and Protestant high clergy against the bitter opposition of the Smallholders and Social Democratic parties and the conservative followers of Count István Bethlen, enacted Hungary's second anti-Jewish law in eighteen years. Count Bethlen argued to no avail that "...there is one thing that is obvious to me: if a *Gleichschaltung* [forced alignment] of political life takes place in Hungary in terms of the ideas of the extreme right, then we shall end up as the servants of Germany and not her friends. That will be the end of an independent Hungarian foreign policy."[1] Bethlen's proclamation would turn out to be prophetic.

Admiral Miklòs Horthy, regent of Hungary from 1920 to 1944, was himself a model of an idiosyncratic brand of the Hungarian right: an antisemite and fanatical anti-Bolshevik, he also hated Nazi ideology because he felt it just as much of a threat to the social order. He outlawed both the Hungarian Nazis, the Nyilas (Arrow Cross Party) and the Hungarian Communists, but drew on Hungary's homegrown antisemitism to appease Hitler, perhaps preventing a stronger Nazi movement from taking over in his country. In the May 1939 elections the Arrow Cross party had won more than 25 per cent of the vote and thirty seats in the Hungarian parliament. Jews constituted a quarter of the population of Budapest, and Hungarian antisemitism was less race-hatred and more smoldering resentment against both the wealth and influence of the highly assimilated Jews and the communist Jews. The strong presence of Jews in the communist leadership internationally and in Hungary itself was an important factor in Hungarian anti-communism. Many Hungarians believed that it was the Jews and their murderous Bolshevik Béla Kun, founder of the Hungarian Communist Party and leader of the 1919 Hungarian communist government's Revolutionary Governing Council, who had cost Hungary its territories in the first place.

---

1   Tibor Frank, *Discussing Hitler: Advisers of U.S. Diplomacy in Central Europe, 1934–1941* (Budapest; New York: Central European University Press, 2003), 47, from Parliamentary Committee documents, Hungarian National Archives, xix: 341–342, as quoted in György Ránki: *Emlékiratok és valóság Magyarország második világháborús szerepéröl* (Budapest: Kossuth, 1964, 46).

~

Once Zuzana, Arthur, Victor and Leah were across the border, Sermer headed to her aunt Ethel's home in Budapest and was delighted to be reunited with family. She obtained false identification papers in the Polish Catholic name of Helena Smutek and worked with a tutor to strengthen her language skills in French. Her facility with languages would prove vital to her survival, even though her tutor turned out to be a traitor.

In March 1944, the delicate balance that Hungary had kept with Germany came abruptly to an end. Hungary had been profiting handsomely from the extraction of Jewish assets; it had passed its restrictions early and enforced them severely. Although the government had resisted mass deportations, in August 1941 thousands of Orthodox Jews who had flooded in from the re-annexed countries were forcibly repatriated to the Ukraine and slaughtered by the SS as "stateless" persons. Six months later, in January 1942, the Hungarian police murdered more than eight hundred Jews in Novi Sad, part of Nazi-occupied northern Yugoslavia annexed to Hungary. Hungary had prospered as Germany's supplier, but early in 1944 Horthy realized that Germany was going to lose the war and tried to negotiate with the Allies to extract Hungary from its pact with Germany. Outfoxed by Hitler, however, Horthy could only watch as Germany invaded their last ally. As Sermer writes, "Not surprisingly, yet somehow still shocking to us, the German army marched into Hungary on March 19, 1944, accompanied by the Gestapo and the SS. The Gestapo officers were especially bloodthirsty and keen to replenish their bottomless coffers to satisfy their growing taste for luxury items."

Following the German invasion of Hungary, the Csepel works, the largest armaments factory in Hungary, was appropriated from the Manfred Weiss family and the owners escaped with their lives to Portugal. In the six weeks between the beginning of May and mid-June, the Hungarian government under Horthy carried out the swiftest deportations of any country in Europe. Between May 15 and July 9, more than 437,000 people were deported and all but about 10,000 to 15,000 were sent to Auschwitz-Birkenau. The machinery designed to round up and murder the Jews of Europe was well oiled and if the Germans were going to lose the war, they were at least determined to win the battle of the "Final Solution."

Many Hungarians were enthusiastic participants in these actions and the gendarmes cleansed the country, though these men were posted to places other than their own locales – as had been the practice in Slovakia – so they didn't have to deal with their friends and neighbours. Also similar to Slovakia, the army battalions of forced labour were some of the safer places to be as long as you weren't shipped to the Eastern Front.

Unleashed, the Arrow Cross began to terrorize the Jewish community of Budapest, which had been rounded up in a concentrated ghetto of 200,000 people. Between deportation, labour camps, Hungarian gendarmes and Arrow Cross raids, only 70,000 Jews survived in the ghetto and about another 20,000 in specially marked houses outside the ghetto, the so-called yellow star houses, which had been granted diplomatic immunity. The Budapest Jews were the last remaining Jewish community in continental Europe. Realizing that things were going to end badly in Hungary, Zuzana, Victor and Arthur started looking for a way back to Slovakia, but were arrested before they could get away. Sermer, afraid of being beaten, admitted that she was Jewish, also exposing her now-fiancé Arthur and his brother, and the three were sent to labour camps in the Csepel works and a brick factory in Békásmegyer on the Danube that, according to Sermer, housed 30,000 Jews awaiting deportation to Poland. Arthur was determined that neither Zuzana nor Victor nor he would leave the brick factory in a cattle car. His confidence and quick thinking would save both himself and Zuzana time and time again as they worked their way out of one imminently fatal situation only to find themselves in another.

Finally released and posing as Polish gentiles, Zuzana and Arthur lived more or less under the radar in Budapest, but they were in a dangerously unstable political state. As Soviet troops began to occupy more Hungarian territory, advancing on Budapest, a desperate Horthy signed an armistice with Moscow. Publicly announced on the radio, Hungarians celebrated the end of the war, but it was short-lived; Horthy was kidnapped by the Germans and forced to abdicate. On October 15, 1944, Ferenc Szálasi, leader of the fascist Arrow Cross Party, was installed as head of the country, though he was little more than a puppet of the Germans. He ruled by terror. The roundups and the deportations were restarted and the Arrow Cross shot thousands of Jews on the edge of the Danube. Sermer was again arrested but this time played dumb, pretending not to speak Hungarian.

The couple ended up renting a room from a woman loyal to Szálasi whose son was on the Eastern Front fighting the "Jewish" Communists. Hiding in plain sight was precarious and they found an odd kind of safety in the anonymity of a bomb shelter where they waited out the relentless bombardment of Budapest now surrounded by the Soviet army and defended by the German and Hungarian armies. The Red Army liberated Hungary and the country declared war on Germany on December 31, 1944. On January 18, 1945, Zuzana and Arthur emerged from the shelter to silent streets along with the rest of the inhabitants of the city. Their war was over, though they were still not out of danger.

By the spring of 1945 Zuzana and Arthur were ready to leave Budapest, somewhat sadly, to return to Slovakia. On the platform waiting for a late train to take them back to their country, they were reunited with Victor, who had come to Hungary to search for them. From him they learned the fate of Zuzana's father in the aftermath of the Slovak National Uprising. The outbreak of the uprising at the end of August 1944 had triggered a second wave of roundups and deportations and of the remaining 24,000 Jews in Slovakia, less than 10,000 survived. Arthur's family was gone.

Returning to Humenné, Sermer collected what remained of her family's belongings, what little had been saved by neighbours, particularly photographs. Only one photograph of her father – a man who observed God's strictures against idolatrous imagery – existed: his passport photo. Most of the classmates in her school photos had been killed, but a lucky few had made it out alive. Like so many Jews who returned home after the war, Sermer discovered that Humenné was home no longer. "Hardly anyone remained in their native towns," she writes. "It would have been like witnessing the past at every turn."

On April 5, 1945, the Czechoslovak Republic was reconstituted as a common state of two equal nations. Just over 10,000 returning Jews had registered with the Jewish communities. Out of a total of 80,614 who had been deported, 6,392 had died in Theresienstadt and 64,172 had been murdered in the death camps. Of the Jews who had not been deported, 5,201 had either been executed, committed suicide or died a natural death. Only 2,803 Jews who had not been deported were still alive in Bohemia and Moravia, most of them partners of mixed marriages. The returnees in the regions of southeastern Poland, the Ukraine and eastern Czechoslovakia were further terrorized by roving bands of *banderas*, a loose organization of mostly army deserters and Ukrainian nationalists named after Stepan Bandera, the controversial leader of the anti-communist Ukrainian nationalist movement.

Zuzana and Arthur married in Humenné but danger and loss moved them to Bratislava, a city in the southwest of Slovakia where they remained for the next twenty-three years.

In her memoir, Sermer reflects on the difference between looking back and looking ahead. She and her husband didn't turn their backs on the past, but neither did they dwell there, knowing that an element of successful survival is the ability to live in the present. Despite their best efforts, however, history continued to erupt in the stories of old friends and the repayment of old debts. As Sermer pieces together these detailed stories, sometimes many years after the fact, we are accosted with the many horrors that Sermer herself was lucky enough to escape.

The Sermers started a family, had four children and lived life fully in communist Slovakia, a regime established shortly after the Communists took political power early in 1948. It was a regime that discouraged racial, national or ethnic identification, and though Zuzana and her family, like so many of the remaining Jews in communist Eastern Europe, didn't hide, maintaining some sense of Jewish community, neither did they advertise their Jewish past. Their children grew up without any sense of Jewish ritual.

This period of relative calm and prosperity was broken once again when the Soviets occupied Czechoslovakia in August 1968. The 1960 constitutional law had declared socialism the economic system of the newly renamed Czechoslovak Socialist Republic. Alexander Dubček, who advocated a reform program called "socialism with a human face," led the new reformist wing of the Czechoslovak Communist Party. But following the Hungarian revolution of 1956, the Soviets were in no mood to tolerate liberalization and the five member states of the Warsaw Pact (the USSR, East Germany, Poland, Hungary and Bulgaria) entered the country on August 21, 1968, with approximately 500,000 soldiers, 2,000 cannons, 800 air force planes and 6,000 tanks and crushed the Prague Spring. The Sermer family fled again, this time to Vienna, with nothing more than train tickets and suitcases packed for a short holiday. Sermer gives us no explanation for their flight, but one can surmise that a combination of a sensitivity to shifts in the political weather and the opportunity for escape from an oppressive regime, combined with a rise in antisemitism, propelled them to leave. Thousands of Czechs fled the country, including 3,400 Jews. From Vienna the Sermers immigrated to Canada in October 1968.

From the safety of Canada, where Sermer and her family were able to re-establish their Jewish lives, Sermer reflects on the miracles of her survival. On the occasion of her grandson's bar mitzvah, a Torah scroll saved by circuitous means from a decimated Czech community serves as emblematic of survival and continuity, as does Sermer's story itself. In the acrylics that she still paints, she infuses the colours of life and loss, and the miracle of regeneration in the face of near-annihilation.

Julia Creet
York University
2012

SOURCES AND FURTHER READING

Braham, Randolph L. *The Politics of Genocide: the Holocaust in Hungary*. Condensed. Detroit, MI; Washington, DC: Wayne State University Press; United States Holocaust Memorial Museum, 2000. Print.

Braham, Randolph L., Scott Miller, and United States Holocaust Memorial Museum. *The Nazis' Last Victims: the Holocaust in Hungary*. Detroit: Wayne State University Press, 1998. Print.

Cesarani, David. *Genocide and Rescue: The Holocaust in Hungary 1944*. Oxford; New York: Berg, 1997. Print.

Conway, John S. "The Churches, the Slovak State and the Jews 1939–1945." *The Slavonic and East European Review* 52.126 (1974): 85–112. Web. August 7 2012.

Frank, Tibor. *Discussing Hitler: Advisers of U.S. Diplomacy in Central Europe, 1934–1941*. Budapest; New York: Central European University Press, 2003. Print.

Komoroczy, Geza, Viktoria Pusztai, and Andrea Strbik. *Jewish Budapest: Monuments, Rites, History*. Ed. Kinga Frojimovics. Central European University Press, 1999. Print.

Lendvai, Paul. *The Hungarians: A Thousand Years of Victory in Defeat*. Princeton University Press, 2004. Print.

Rothkirchen, Livia. *The Jews of Bohemia and Moravia: Facing the Holocaust*. University of Nebraska Press, 2006. Print.

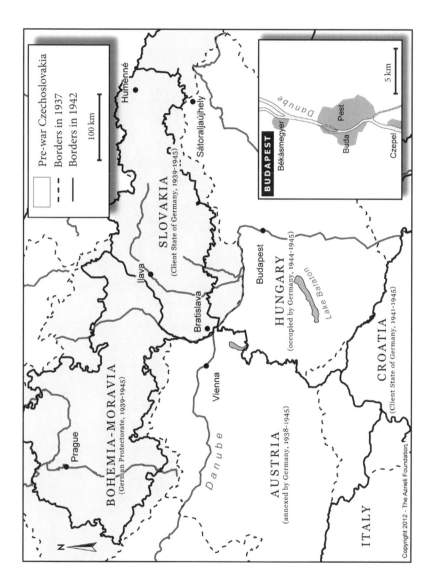

Pre-war Czechoslovakia
Borders in 1937
Borders in 1942

100 km

Humenné

Sátoraljaújhely

SLOVAKIA
(Client State of Germany, 1939-1945)

Ilava

Bratislava

Budapest

HUNGARY
(occupied by Germany, 1944-1945)

Lake Balaton

BOHEMIA-MORAVIA
(German Protectorate, 1939-1945)

Prague

Vienna

Danube

AUSTRIA
(annexed by Germany, 1938-1945)

CROATIA
(Client State of Germany, 1941-1945)

ITALY

N

Copyright 2012 - The Azrieli Foundation.

BUDAPEST

Danube

Békásmegyer

Pest

Buda

Czepel

5 km

Zuzana Sermer's Family Tree*

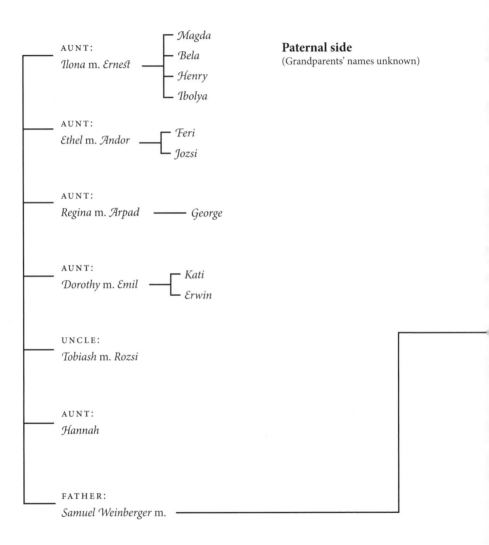

AUNT:
Ilona m. Ernest

- Magda
- Bela
- Henry
- Ibolya

AUNT:
Ethel m. Andor

- Feri
- Jozsi

AUNT:
Regina m. Arpad ——— George

AUNT:
Dorothy m. Emil

- Kati
- Erwin

UNCLE:
Tobiash m. Rozsi

AUNT:
Hannah

FATHER:
Samuel Weinberger m.

Paternal side
(Grandparents' names unknown)

UNCLE:
Dov m. Name Unknown

AUNT:
Rose

Maternal side
(Grandparents' names unknown)

AUNT:
Fanny m. Kalman — Rose
— Josephine

AUNT:
Irene m. William — Magda

UNCLE:
David

AUNT:
Lina m. Jack — 2 Children

MOTHER:
Vilma Stern — *Zuzana Weinberger*; m. Arthur Sermer
born 1924

DAUGHTER:
Tamara m. Victor — Nicole
remarried Bruce — Mark

SON:
Paul m. Susan — Tanya
— Julie

SON:
Michael m. Margi — David
— Becky

SON:
Matthew m. Lillian — Corey
— Jessica

To Tamarka, Palko, Miško and Mako

I am grateful to my daughter-in-law Susan Sermer for carefully reading the original manuscript and providing valuable comments.

Some names (other than those of my family members) have been changed to protect the privacy of the people involved and their families.

Author's Preface

As I retrace the extraordinary events of my youth, I must confess that my mind is absorbed by the past. More than fifty years have gone by since World War II and I still review that time, searching for explanations for the incredible circumstances that contributed to my survival.

How can I explain the unexplainable? There were so many factors that enabled me to be here to examine them today: luck, coincidence and occurrences that I have come to think of as miracles. My parents' love, my bold naïveté, the courage and determination of my fiancé – all of these things played a part in my being here to recall my own story. I was fortunate that so many factors worked in my favour.

At some point, when I reflected about the past, I realized that I did not want to carry the events in my life to my grave. I have always enjoyed writing – in my early teenage years I wrote poems, essays and even lyrics to music. In 1955, ten years after the war, when at last I studied for my long overdue high school diploma, I read my work to my literature class. The stories and ideas came from deep within me and I couldn't rest until I saw the words on a page in front of me.

My words always had a moral, a bottom line. It never occurred to me to simply write for the sake of writing. After the war, while the Communist system in Slovakia was emerging, there was ample food for thought and topics to write about. My articles appeared in a variety of magazines and newspapers. I wrote about individuals who had done good deeds and about doing the right thing. I observed the consequences of inadvertent human errors and the way different people handled their harsh economic and political situations. I also began writing articles from my perspective as a mother, advising others how to help children avoid bad eating habits and on ways to balance play time with study time.

Following these productive years of raising children and writing, my family fled Communist Slovakia after the Soviets invaded in 1968, and immigrated to Canada that same year. Our four children, Tamara, Paul, Michael and Matthew, completed their education, married and gave us eight beautiful grandchildren. My husband, Arthur, and I now find ourselves enjoying our golden years, both of us in relatively good health but looking ahead to the future less and less. As one might expect, our social circle has diminished and the social life that once filled our calendar has been replaced by doctors' appointments and funerals. But I hope that as we age, we will become less demanding and more modest.

Given my penchant for writing earlier in my life, it was only natural that I should eventually have the urge to write down my life story. The desire to create and be productive was deeply rooted within me during those horrific years of war. A spiritual strength and conviction coursed through my blood. And while the creative spark was, of necessity, on hold for a long period of time, now the time to share my story is finally right.

When I began to tell friends and acquaintances that I was writing a book, I was met with a variety of reactions. One question they repeatedly asked was: What language was I writing in? This was a legitimate question, as English is clearly not my first language. In fact, it is not even my second language! My answer, always, was that I would write in English. I didn't feel I needed to write in my mother tongue – Hungarian – and have the work translated. I was proud to be able to write in English. Their attention then, inevitably, turned to the subject matter. What was I writing about? This wasn't a surprising question either because I had written on such a wide variety of topics after the war. To this I simply replied, "I am writing about the war. I am telling the story of my miraculous survival."

Some of my friends who survived the Holocaust pointed out that I am not the only one who has a story to tell. "Oh, THAT!" one survivor told me. "I could write about it too. I could talk about it for hours. Remember when I got out of the ghetto and I didn't have a valid ID? But who is strong enough to tell these stories?" Another said, "Can you tell me who really cares, now, after more than fifty years? Who gives a damn about what happened to us? I spent a day being video-taped talking about my war story for Spielberg's Shoah Foundation.[1] So what?"

I know other survivors who also feel this way. Holocaust education has only recently become a priority, which is hard for many of us to accept. Why did it take so long? Some said it would have been emotionally damaging to young students, but that answer wasn't good enough for most of us. We wondered what could be more important than teaching about the slaughter of the Jews of Europe. Aren't the long-term consequences relevant to us all? I feel that it's crucial for future generations to learn about the injustices we suffered during the Holocaust and to learn that they must never succumb to prejudice and brutality. There are also lessons to be garnered from the war about fighting for one's rights. If we could gain one thing from World War II, I wish it would be an understanding of the need to eliminate hatred of all kinds, which still exists today.

At a time when more and more Holocaust literature has been

---

[1] For information on the USC Shoah Foundation Institute, as well as on other major organizations; significant historical events and people; geographical locations; religious and cultural terms; and foreign-language words and expressions contained in the text, please see the glossary.

published, some may wonder if it is too much. "Who can read it all?" one friend asked me. But is there really a glut of such books on the market? How can a handful of Holocaust survivors telling their stories be too much? The conclusion I have reached is that these are our stories to tell, and tell them we should. It is up to others to decide if they will read them – my hope is that they will.

In telling my story of survival and the stories of others I knew and met, I have tried not to sink to unbearable depths. There were horrific events in these experiences, but often there was also hope. Although the subject matter is heavy, it is not my intention to reduce readers to tears. My aim is to enlighten those who want to listen and to share the thread of hope that has woven through my life, hope that has been based on how I perceive the world around me.

It's not easy to explain myself to others. My feeling is that as long as I hang on to my core beliefs, I am not lost. Throughout my ordeals during the war, my hope and optimism were a guiding force that helped me to survive. Even today, this outlook helps me get through the uphill climbs in my life. My experiences have also led me to believe in fate. I must, otherwise my analysis of the events of my life would not make sense. However, hope and fate alone are not enough; we must also always be prepared to help ourselves. Thank God, in most situations, we are able to do so.

Still, I wonder what force was protecting me during the war. I have to believe that those of us who survived were protected by an invisible, good force. I don't mean to present my life as a special case – it was not special. But when millions lost their lives, including my father and many other members of my family, it is an extraordinary thing to have survived.

Many of us have tried to lock away the memories, but it is important that we tell our stories. I want to put on record the fateful events that enabled me, and others whom I know, to endure. To do so, I present to you this survival kit. I hope that my memoir will contribute to the body of knowledge about the Holocaust and that my family and others will gain from these lessons. We must learn from the past that we always need to be on alert. This, not vengeance, is our best weapon.

Zuzana Sermer
1999

My Hometown

I was born in the town of Humenné, Slovakia on August 29, 1924. The town is located at the foot of the Carpathian Mountains and the climate is perfect – summers are never humid and winters are moderate. When I was growing up, just under half of the town's six thousand residents were Jewish, and the other half was almost all Roman Catholic, mixed with small communities of Lutherans, Greek Orthodox and Roma. Today, approximately 90 per cent of Humenné's inhabitants are Slovak Catholics and most of the rest are Greek-Orthodox Ruthenians. There are also small groups of Roma and a tiny pocket of Hungarians. Only a handful of Jews remain.

The first known written records about Humenné date back to the year 1317. I know this because of an invitation I received in the late 1990s from the city's mayor. I must admit that I was caught by surprise – firstly, that the city of my birth has had such a long history, and secondly, that I was remembered there after living away for more than fifty years. Accompanying the invitation to an event in my hometown was a letter explaining that this day would also commemorate the martyrs of World War II.

Part of the event's program involved the dedication of a plaque honouring Jewish "co-citizens." I found that word amusing because I remember how Jews were politely called "co-citizens" by government officials and journalists during the Communist era who had worked for the fascist regime in Slovakia during the war and then continued, under Communist rule, to hold high positions in the government or media. By erecting a dense wall of fog to hide details of their wartime pasts, they started their lives anew after 1945 with clean slates.

Why "co-citizens"? No one ever talked about Catholic co-citizens. Why make a distinction at all when everyone has the same ID cards, birth certificates and citizenship – all issued by the same government – and when everyone must obey the law of the land? Before the war, Jews formed an integral part of the citizenry of Slovakia. I wondered why this term "co-citizen" was still alive in Humenné.

I sense that the past is not completely forgotten in my old home-town. The mayor's letter stressed that the town's "Jewish religious community" had suggested inviting me. I wondered who they were. I know of only one Jewish family still living in Humenné, the family of one of my childhood girlfriends, and I doubt that there would be more than fifteen other Jews currently living there. How frustrating it must have been for the local officials to try to find survivors after more than half a century!

The government took too long to openly admit the tragedy of Slovakia's Jews and take an official position, and Jews are still on the margins of history in this region. For example, when I was last at the monument that marks the mass grave in Kremnička, Slovakia that contains the remains of close to eight hundred people killed by German soldiers in November 1944 during the Slovak National Uprising, there wasn't a word about Jewish victims. Almost 50 per cent of those killed there were Jewish, yet engraved on the tall grey-black marble tomb were only the names of nationalities such as Slovak, Czech, Russian and Roma, and also the description "women and children." I've heard, thankfully, that this monument has since been changed, to reflect the reality of how many Jews were killed there.

I didn't go to Humenné for that commemorative event. At seventy-two years old, it would have been too difficult and I needed to avoid stress as much as possible. Nonetheless, I was thrilled to receive the invitation from the mayor.

The last time I visited Humenné was in 1992, one year before my old country, Czechoslovakia, broke peacefully into two unequal halves: the Czech Republic and Slovakia. This separation broke many people's hearts. After World War I, when the Austro-Hungarian Empire collapsed, the first Republic of Czechoslovakia was formed. Czechoslovakia was a pearl of democracy among the bordering countries and in central Europe more generally. The first time the country was violently broken was in September 1938, when Hitler swallowed its western border regions of Bohemia, Moravia and Silesia, then known as the Sudetenland, thus enlarging Germany's territory. Then, in March 1939, Hitler took over the central region, establishing the Protectorate of Bohemia and Moravia and proclaiming Slovakia an independent state under the protective wings of Germany. This puppet regime followed Hitler loyally until the end of the war. In 1993, the country of my happy childhood was broken for the third time – forever, I assume.

At the time of my visit, Humenné felt strange and unrecognizable. The only familiar landmark was the majestic castle that for several hundred years belonged to the counts Andrássy, famed aristocrats of the Austro-Hungarian Empire. Not only had Humenné been completely rebuilt, but it had also expanded, amalgamating the surrounding villages. Many streets had completely disappeared and had been replaced by wider, larger thoroughfares. New apartment buildings were built to accommodate the influx of young people from the surrounding villages who left their family's farms behind to find work in the city. Many more people had moved into the city from fairly distant towns and villages and the population ballooned to forty thousand.

The remarkable physical expansion of the city was even more noticeable when I visited my mother's grave. In my memory, the Jewish cemetery was at least two kilometres away from the town, but now it was close to one of the city streets. It was a neglected, sombre place. Before the war, the cemetery was never neglected. I was surprised, but I am not sure why. I couldn't have expected that Humenné would remain unchanged after I painfully abandoned it so long ago.

My memories transported me to the pre-war Humenné of my youth, when the Jewish population had numbered almost three thousand. I walked down Masaryk Street, also called Main Street, where I had first lived with my family. It was among the few unchanged streets. Before the war, our two-storey building contained three apartments – one upstairs and two downstairs. I lived with my parents in one of the main-floor apartments, a spacious two-bedroom, roomy enough for two families. The woman who owned the house lived upstairs. Her late husband had been in banking and her bachelor son was a medical student. She also had two daughters and one of them was married with two children and owned a drugstore.

During the peaceful times of the first Czechoslovak republic, my landlady's family was typical of upper middle-class Jewish society. Many Jewish families owned homes and businesses. They emphasized education for their children and encouraged extracurricular activities, depending on the youngsters' interests and talents. Their social life revolved around families of the same status and they tended not to mix with the lower strata of society. They were more inclined to befriend their non-Jewish peers. It seemed that the question of "How important am I?" or "Whom (or what) do I represent?" was crucial for people. The guiding principle was that everyone was out for him or herself. A popular proverb was: "Money talks; a dog barks."

This was not the way of life for more observant Jews or for Jewish society as a whole. The deeply religious Orthodox Jews were a large and separate entity. Their ancestors had settled in Slovakia more than a hundred years earlier, mostly immigrating from Poland. They were mainly concentrated in villages and small towns and held on to their identity fiercely. Influenced by Polish Hasidism, with its famous rabbis, many in this group believed in rabbis' prophecies and in their almost superhuman qualities. The rabbis' teachings, along with the Torah, led these very religious Jews to expect the arrival of the Messiah and they lived in anticipation of that event. Everything worldly was beyond their interest. Life concentrated on the study of the Torah, the core Jewish scripture, and the ancient rabbinic text called the Talmud, both of which served as the guiding principle of their lives.

Orthodox fathers ensured that their sons began their religious studies at the age of four, from early in the morning until sunset. The sons later attended separate religious schools in the mornings or evenings, at times that didn't conflict with public schools. These studies filled childhood, adolescence, marriage and family life. Parents prepared their sons to become brilliant scholars and their daughters to become dutiful wives whose primary duty was to have children. Women were to become queens of their households and obey Jewish law.

Orthodox families willingly isolated themselves from other Jews by their way of life. Their place of worship was also separate and an outsider would rightly assume that they avoided liberal or even secular influences. This profile would fit religious families in many of the towns and cities of the eastern regions of Slovakia at the time. Orthodox Jews concentrated on their religious lives regardless of where they were living.

A third social group, comprised of a fairly small number of professionals – physicians, lawyers, pharmacists and some engineers – were the "elite" of Jewish society in Humenné and were very wealthy by the standards of eastern Slovakia in the 1930s. Everyone looked up to these privileged people who appeared immune to daily hardships. Few in number but substantial in influence, they led highly isolated, almost aristocratic lives. In fact, the average person knew little about this elite group. The wealthy Jews weren't very religious and they mingled with Hungarian high society, but they seldom intermarried with non-Jews. Some attended the synagogue twice a year during the high holidays of Rosh Hashanah, the Jewish new year, and Yom Kippur, the day of atonement; others attended services on March 7, the birthday of president and founder of Czechoslovakia Tomáš Garrigue Masaryk, or on October 28, the anniversary of the proclamation of the Czechoslovak republic in 1918.

The wealthy were usually generous and charitable to the less fortunate, in line with the humanitarian approach of Jewish teachings that highly values good deeds. There weren't any Slovaks of equivalent status, at least not in Humenné. The Slovaks under the Austro-Hungarian monarchy, and later in Czechoslovakia, were without opportunities, oppressed by the Hungarians and then by the Czechs.

The fourth and last Jewish social group in pre-war Humenné consisted of us average eastern Slovak Jews, from very poor to middle class, who didn't fit into any of the other three categories. We worked for our daily bread – some with ease, some not so easily – and struggled to achieve what earlier generations had been unable to attain: recognition and a better future for our children while facing a wide variety of economic conditions. Many families tried hard to make ends meet and to maintain their dignity.

$\sim$

All the Jews of Humenné had a governing body called the Jewish Religious Community that dealt with religious, educational and sometimes even legal needs. It had been set up in the nineteenth century to help feudal landowners collect taxes from Jewish people. During my childhood there was a membership fee for this body, also called a religious tax.

In the Jewish community of Humenné, people born before World War I associated their cultural and intellectual background with Hungary. They often spoke Hungarian and maintained allegiance to the Austro-Hungarian Empire. In 1918, after the Habsburg monarchy collapsed and the First Czechoslovak Republic was established, all minorities could register in whichever nationality they preferred, regardless of their language. Three years later, the first census showed that many Jews self-identified as Hungarian. This was not unusual for the Jews of Humenné, who had spent most of their lives under the old Austro-Hungarian monarchy, even if they were born on Slovak soil. Almost a decade later, however, more Jews proclaimed themselves to be Slovak than Hungarian. The Orthodox Jews stuck to identifying themselves as Jewish, although they preferred to be categorized as a religious community rather than as a national or ethnic group.

In my family, my mother tongue was Hungarian and my parents subscribed to a Hungarian daily newspaper mailed to us from Košice, a town in eastern Slovakia. It was more natural for them to read Hungarian than Slovak because they usually spoke in Zemplín, an eastern Slovak dialect that no newspaper used, and their knowledge of commonly spoken Slovak was very poor.

We all adjusted to the new conditions of the republic, which in my opinion were more favourable and much freer. In school we had to learn the new official language (Slovak), which was required by the state.

The new generation of Jews born into independent Czechoslovakia were fully committed citizens. We lived under a genuine democracy guided by our beloved president Masaryk, who was respected around the world and nicknamed "the philosopher on the throne." We fondly called him "our father" as we used to sing, "Old father of ours, your head is white; as long as you live, nothing bad can happen to us." He was often considered a hero to the Jews – the guarantor of our democracy, peace and freedom. This image dated back to 1899, in the days of the Austro-Hungarian Empire, when Masaryk, who was a university professor at the time, had openly defended a young Jewish man, Leopold Hilsner, who had been accused of a ritual murder and sentenced to death. This case was known as The Polná Affair, after the town closest to where the crime had been committed. Hilsner had allegedly killed a young Christian girl to get her blood, which was supposedly needed to observe the Passover holiday. This medieval myth, kept alive by antisemites, stirred up anti-Jewish feelings with devastating consequences for Czech Jews. But Masaryk considered the accusation that Jews used Christian blood for their rituals to be an insult to Czech intelligence. Under the weight of Masaryk's influence as well as a legal appeal, Hilsner was retried. He was still found guilty but his sentence was reduced to life imprisonment. Finally, just before the birth of independent Czechoslovakia, he was pardoned and granted his freedom.

Czechoslovakia's national coat of arms bore the motto: "Truth will prevail." Under Masaryk's leadership, everyone, including Jews, could freely express their beliefs – political, national or religious. I think if Czechoslovakia had been able to stay in its initial shape, not ruined by Hitler's war, this civilized, industrious country would have been, as it was then, a model for all the world.

Many Slovaks, however, were not fond of Masaryk's regime. They accused the Czechs of colonialism and felt that they were not being treated equally. Even their sport institutions were separate. The Czech sport organization, Sokol, was all over the country whereas the Slovak equivalent, Orol, was only on Slovak land. Czechs also held all the important regional, educational and military positions all over the country. In reaction to the inadequacy of Slovak representation in governing bodies, Slovak nationalists formed political parties, reflecting their disagreement with the Czech status quo.

Hungarians living in Slovakia were no fonder of Masaryk's government. In 1920, the Treaty of Trianon, which split up the old Austro-Hungarian Empire and established the borders of the new state of Czechoslovakia, had added more than a million people of Hungarian nationality to Slovakia's three million native Slovaks. This significant reduction of Hungary's borders was a blow to the government in Budapest.

Masaryk left office in 1935. He passed away on September 14, 1937, at the age of eighty-seven. I will never forget those sombre days at school; I was thirteen years old and I cried as if I had lost a parent.

～

During my childhood, Jews were an integral part of the population and we always interacted with the non-Jewish half of the community. We lived together in mixed neighbourhoods and we depended on our neighbours and on good relations between our communities. The youngsters spent a lot of time together and mingled on Masaryk Street, the main thoroughfare. We never fought for religious reasons.

Most shop owners on Masaryk Street were Jewish. One could tell since all the shops closed when the Sabbath arrived. Public elementary and junior high schools closed on Saturdays and Sundays, even though the working week was six days, not five. Only in secondary education was attendance on Saturday compulsory.

Many Czech families lived in Humenné and quite a few of them helped to fill the shortage of teachers in Slovak schools. They presented and taught Czech culture and literature and we read many Czech books, since they were well-written or translated, in good supply, and available in many genres, such as biography, history and classic literature.

We were happy with the status quo of Jewish existence in democratic Czechoslovakia, although Jews were not settled equally all over the country. Jews in western regions such as Bohemia and Moravia were fewer in number than in Slovakia, the eastern part of the republic. Czech Jews were also generally less observant and more assimilated than Slovakian Jews. I suppose that was the result of a number of circumstances. Bohemia had a large German population, many of whom were well-educated. The Czechs, too, were very well-educated in both the sciences and humanities and highly accomplished in ethics, politics and civics. Jews living in the western region were able to take advantage of the superb education and wonderful literature, music and technology, and to participate in the cultural life of the nation.

The Jews of Slovakia, in contrast, were some years behind the times. Slovakia did not have the wealth of resources available in Bohemia and Moravia, mainly because hundreds of years of Slovak oppression under the Austro-Hungarian Empire had caused a shortage of industry, economic opportunities and experienced teachers.

I doubt that the Jewish way of life in Humenné was unique – it must have been a common pattern for Jewish communities following the Enlightenment period during the late eighteenth and nineteenth centuries, when Jews were granted political rights. By 1921, Jews had achieved a relatively equal status under the law. All that was to change dramatically during the coming years of war.

Family Roots

At the Holocaust Centre in Toronto, there is a memorial where my parents' names are among the many who perished. Although my parents didn't survive the war, they are an essential part of my survival kit and I continue to pass on their legacy. My father, especially, had a great influence on me. It has been more than sixty years since I last saw him, but he is still a part of my heart and soul and that of my children, my eight grandchildren and, God willing, a part of generations yet to come.

My father's name was Samuel Weinberger. He was born in 1891 – I'm not sure exactly where – and he was twenty-three years old when his four-year career as a soldier began in 1914. It was the start of World War I and he was obliged to defend the great Austro-Hungarian monarchy. He was assigned to Udine, Italy, a city located south of the magnificent Dolomites mountain range and northwest of Venice. It must have been a nice place to live in times of peace. No places are nice in war.

Papa was not trained to load or handle firearms; instead he was taught to manage the telegraphs. My mother and I used to tease him, saying that it was because of him that the monarchy lost the war, yet he was comforted by the knowledge that he had never had to use a gun. My father was special, a man with no enemies, who was admired by many for his kind and noble heart. While walking the streets of

Humenné, my father could always be seen politely holding his hat in his hand as he greeted people. His gentle, refined personality created a warm feeling around him and he had a positive, almost healing effect on others. My father was respected for his honesty and his faithfulness to our family and friends. Everyone in our family adored him.

I'm not sure exactly when my father moved to Humenné, but I know that he married my mother, Vilma, there in 1921. My mother's family, the Sterns, had lived in the town for many generations. I loved our town. It felt as though I knew and was known to everyone. Humenné was, for me, the centre of the universe and I felt secure and happy there. Although my family didn't have a great deal of money, my father – a dairy merchant – was a good provider. We lived through the Great Depression and between two world wars – the worst of economic and political times – yet, until the Nazis invaded, I was never deprived of the basic comforts of life.

As an only child, I was very precious to my parents and maybe even a little bit spoiled. But when I was eleven years old, my mother was diagnosed with congestive heart failure and was bedridden. Until then, I had had quite a happy childhood. My father was patient and extraordinarily loving throughout the painful, difficult years of her prolonged illness. My mother was the youngest of seven children and before I was born, Mama's siblings had scattered all over the world. Her brother Dov and her sister Rose both immigrated to the United States. We occasionally received birthday presents from Aunt Rose, which were always shared among our extended family. Sadly, she passed away in August of 1968, only one month before I arrived in North America, so I never had the opportunity to meet her, nor did I ever meet Dov. My mother's two sisters Fanny and Irene, as well as her brother David, lived in Budapest. We saw them in the summertime during my school holidays when we vacationed in Budapest or when they came to visit us in Humenné.

When my mother was three years old, her eldest sister, Lina, got engaged to Jack, who was from an area near Belgrade, which was then part of the Austro-Hungarian Empire and later of Yugoslavia. My mother told me of her recollections of the wedding, which took place in Humenné. The wedding party was seated at the dinner table, waiting for the meal. My mother sat at the very end of the long table, and at the head of the table were the bride and groom. The food was served and everyone began to eat except for my mother. She was asked, "Why aren't you eating, Vilma?" Loud and clear so that all could hear her, my mother announced that she wanted the same shiny silver fork as the groom. She got her fork and everyone laughed. My mother was a pretty woman – tall, with dark brown hair, a fair complexion and light green eyes. I imagine she must have been a very cute little girl.

My mother's siblings in Budapest gave me many gifts, most often outfits for special occasions. Not many girls in our town could pride themselves on having dresses from Budapest. I remember one elegant outfit in particular, a very feminine, short-sleeved pink dress that I received when I was eleven. The dress had a matching coat with long sleeves and buttons. I had white shoes, a purse, gloves and hat to go with it. I still remember that outfit fondly. I am wearing it in one of the few pictures I have of life before the Nazis invaded my peaceful town.

I have fond memories of my father's six siblings as well. I didn't know his sister Ilona well, since she lived far away, somewhere in Subcarpathian Rus, but my Aunt Dorothy and her family lived in Humenné and we saw them often. My father's other three sisters had moved to Budapest in the early 1920s and our families had remained very close. His oldest sister, Regina, was married to Arpad and they had a son, George. The next eldest, Ethel, married Andor, a tailor who was a decent man, a good provider and lived for his family. My aunt Ethel was a kind, pleasant woman. She was a responsible mother who lovingly brought up her two sons, Feri and Jozsi, with the highest of standards. Having not had a formal education of her own, my aunt always said, "Education is your safest investment. Nobody can take it away from you." Hannah, my father's youngest sister, never married. Aunt Hannah lived with Ethel and her family. She worked very hard throughout her life in order to help make ends meet.

My father's younger brother, Tobiash, was especially memorable. Uncle Tobiash lived in Strážske, a village not far from Humenné. In the 1920s he married his beloved Rozsi, a match that caused some controversy. Aunt Rozsi had a remarkable passion for jewellery, which caused my father's family to predict that their marriage wouldn't last, although they were very much in love with each other. Rozsi came to the marriage with her own good jewellery and throughout the years Uncle Tobiash lovingly supplied her with more whenever he could.

My uncle made his living by horse-trading. He provided work horses for labour in the field and for pulling carriages. All of the villagers, whether they were farmers, merchants or peasants, knew Uncle Tobiash since each of them required horses at one time or another. They had also all heard him tell the story of his frightening encounter as a youth. Tobiash had been walking on the road near the village when suddenly he heard loud rumbling in the distance. The noise sounded like a combination of rolling thunder and battle cannons and grew louder by the second. As he looked in the direction from which it came, he could see a black box roaring rapidly toward him. He thought it was the devil so he jumped into a roadside ditch, covered his head with his hands and waited. From this vantage point he peeked up as the box sped by him and saw a man sitting inside. This was my uncle's first encounter with an automobile!

One day each month, Uncle Tobiash took his horses to trade at the market being held in the city closest to Strážske. When he had a successful day, he returned home with small gifts of jewellery for Rozsi. They weren't blessed with children and these gifts brought her joy. These were peaceful, simple times.

Once, when Uncle Tobiash was doing business in the city, some unexpected excitement came his way in the form of a letter. Just as my uncle was preparing to head for home, a friend who had a high position in the post office called out to him, breathlessly exclaiming, "I have an envelope for you from America!" When Uncle Tobiash took the envelope he saw that it was addressed to Mr. Tobiash Herman, Number 50, Michalovce.

"My dear friend," said Uncle Tobiash, "I am Tobiash Herman *Weinberger*. I do live at Number 50, but in the village of Strážske." The village of Strážske was within the jurisdiction of the city of Michalovce.

"He simply forgot to write your last name," replied my uncle's friend.

"Who's the sender?" asked my uncle.

"It's from Detroit, USA."

There was no sender's name on the envelope, but it had come from an American bank. Uncle Tobiash was also known as Tobiash Herman. Both were translations from his Hebrew name, Tovyah. With some misgivings, Uncle Tobiash took the envelope and began the journey home. He was too preoccupied to buy any jewellery that day.

Studying the letter with Rozsi, Uncle Tobiash discovered that a Mr. Tobiash Herman had inherited ten thousand US dollars! This is a great deal of money now and it was considered a fortune then. The deceased, a Mr. Stephen Herman, had apparently designated only one beneficiary of his estate, namely, Tobiash Herman. Uncle Tobiash was instructed to submit his birth certificate, his parents' wedding certificate and proof of his relationship to the departed. The letter, a long and complicated document, went on to explain that in the absence of these certificates, witnessed statements would be acceptable. The bank went on to outline the various administrative fees and inheritance charges.

Uncle Tobiash rushed to Humenné and assembled his family to ask if anyone know who this Stephen Herman was. The family met and discussed the question several times, but beyond some guess work, nobody knew for sure. After two months of searching for an answer, Uncle Tobiash was a nervous wreck. One does not get such manna from heaven every day, but it was turning out to be a nightmare. He was beginning to wonder if the devil himself had sent that letter.

Deep inside, Uncle Tobiash didn't believe that the money belonged to him. The name Weinberger was not mentioned anywhere. Yes, perhaps there could have been an error on the envelope, but surely the full name of the beneficiary would have appeared within a document as important as this. He decided to go to the local bank and discuss the matter with experts.

After hearing the story, the bank official looked at my uncle in total disbelief. "Mr. Weinberger, you could have been a very rich man." Uncle Tobiash never forgot this episode. One day he received an unstamped envelope with his full name printed on the front. Upon opening it he found a note inside, handwritten in broken Hungarian. It said, "Everyone gets what he deserves." Along with the note was a banknote for ten US dollars.

If only humankind had more people like my uncle Tobiash. His golden heart and pure conscience was worth a fortune to those who knew him. My uncle Tobiash deserved so much more, more even than the ten thousand dollars that almost came his way.

Uncle Tobiash, along with so many others in my family, left this world as smoke from the chimneys at Auschwitz.

⌒

My father was pious and I grew up in a religious environment. I know it would please Papa now to see his daughter, grandchildren and even great-grandchildren following his path in their commitment to Judaism. This too is part of his legacy, and a part of my survival kit as well.

I was introduced to the basics of Judaism at the age of six. In addition to public school, on Sundays I attended Beth Jacob school for girls, which promoted the philosophy of Agudah, the most religious movement in our town. There we were taught that there was nothing more important than the study of Torah and that only Torah should guide every aspect of our lives. In class I learned about Jewish history, read tales from the Bible and the Torah, and delved into the intricacies of the Hebrew language. My parents were content to have me enrolled there, yet they felt more of an affinity for Mizrachi, a religious Zionist movement.

Both Agudah and Mizrachi were Orthodox religious political movements, but they differed in the ways that they approached Judaism. Agudah taught that the only correct way to live was to spend all possible time studying Torah. They rejected worldly influences that could come between the Jews and Torah. I understand that this remains their philosophy today, both in the Diaspora and in Israel. The Mizrachi movement of my childhood was a Zionist movement that taught that studying Torah and working to develop the Land of Israel as a Jewish homeland went hand in hand. It was a down-to-earth ideology and, at the time, appealed largely to middle-aged people in my town.

At Beth Jacob, my teacher was a tall, skinny young woman. She was the daughter of a highly respected local rabbi and her family, which included numerous sisters and brothers, had a reputation for being very learned. They focused on the study of Torah and often hosted scholars and Jewish intellectuals from all over Central Europe. My teacher was an intelligent woman who had earned her degree in teaching Judaism at a well-known Jewish religious school in Vienna. After my two years at Beth Jacob our paths didn't cross again in Humenné, although we both remained in the town. I remember her as very religious, straightforward and knowledgeable.

After the war, I was surprised to discover that those who came in contact with my former teacher in Auschwitz had formed a different opinion of her. She had been among the first group to be deported from our town to Auschwitz in March 1942 and had become a *Block-älteste* there, a privileged barracks leader who oversaw hundreds of women. Orders were given daily by the SS and she was responsible for seeing that they were carried out. Most of the orders were unpleasant duties, but if the *Blockälteste* did not comply, she risked her own life – to disobey would likely have meant execution on the spot. There were also *Blockältesten* who went above and beyond what was required of them, often in the hope of saving family members or themselves. The impression I was given of my former teacher by those who knew her at Auschwitz was not a flattering one.

After the war, she immigrated to Toronto. When I too came to Toronto in 1968, she visited me, bringing frivolous presents that I put away with other memorabilia. Maybe the years in Auschwitz had brought out a dark side of her personality, but it was clear to me that her deep religious devotion still remained. Fortunately, at the time of her visit, I didn't yet know of her role in the camp during the war. I talked to her with no reservations – after all, she was someone from my childhood who had also survived the horrors of the war.

When I was around eight years old, I left Beth Jacob and became a member of the Mizrachi youth group, Bnei Akiva. The change represented an ideological shift I was unaware of at the time, but it was clear that this was a more comfortable match for my family's outlook. I remained in Bnei Akiva for two or three years, and my parents encouraged me to attend all of its activities. I enjoyed participating and at the same time I learned a great deal. In time I came to feel that the work ethic of Mizrachi was most admirable and noteworthy.

Thinking back on my education, I am struck by how little remains with me from my early Agudah education. My parents' beliefs had a more significant and lasting influence on me.

Mizrachi was only one of the many different Zionist organizations in Humenné. Some members of these groups were idealists who hoped to build a Jewish homeland in British Mandate Palestine. These young people left Humenné for Palestine, relinquishing their own material comforts to ease the financial burden on their families. Others left when the rise of Hitler in the early 1930s suggested an ugly future.

The Lives We Knew

In 1935, when my mother became ill, our lives changed drastically. She had an operation and spent one full year hospitalized in Budapest. In addition to our own situation, Jewish life throughout Europe was deteriorating.

Something dangerous was festering outside our little paradise. We all sensed it. Almost the entire decade before the war had been peaceful in Humenné – at least in my memory. We concentrated on our families and on the little events in our own circles. Since the radio wasn't a regular household item, important world news was announced over the town's loudspeakers. But news arrived to us delayed, often in contradictory or confusing versions. Large, dark, dense clouds were forming under our bright blue skies. We tried to ignore them, but from 1933 onwards, something was always happening to make political discussions heated and the whole country, especially the Jews, was getting jittery.

When Hitler came to power in Germany in 1933, we nevertheless exercised poor judgment. We never guessed that the world was so small. Besides, we weren't pessimists – we all knew that the Germans were considered the most civilized and intelligent people in Europe. We didn't think that they would ever stoop to wickedness or criminal, inhuman acts. We understood quite clearly their post-World War I difficulties, which were mainly economic, but many states had the same problems after the war.

Then, in 1936, the Civil War in Spain caused many of us to grow even more concerned. A fascist revolution in Spain, supported by Hitler! An organized fighting unit loyal to the Spanish republic was soon established and named the International Brigades. Thousands of enthusiasts, supporters of democracy from all over the world, including the Americas, went to Spain to fight fascism. Those volunteers kept our spirits and hopes up. I remember that some soldiers even joined from Humenné.

I will never forget how devastated everybody was when Barcelona fell to the fascists in 1939. I was fourteen then and we young people still hoped that a miracle would save Spain. Some of us approached politics as people say an ostrich reacts to danger – burying our heads in the sand. In any case, we felt we were in no position to help because geographically we were quite far from Spain. We had trusted that the world's democracies would unite and prevent another fascist dictatorship. Obviously our knowledge of the situation – politics, diplomacy, international agreements, military pacts – was totally inadequate and unrealistic. It seems to me that our war started not on September 1, 1939, when Hitler invaded Poland, but many years earlier.

∼

Much of what started to happen to Jews in our country was an echo of the situation for Jews in Germany. In March 1939, after the Nazis invaded Czechoslovakia, an independent Slovak state was established. In reality, it was a fascist puppet state that mirrored Nazi Germany. Its ruling political party – Hlinka's Slovak People's Party – was structured in the same way as the Nazi party. It had its own Gestapo, known as the Hlinka Guard, and its members, like the Gestapo, had sinister black uniforms. The youth in particular, eager to show off their uniforms, marched in the street yelling inflammatory antisemitic slogans. It was astonishing to see how many new members the Hlinka party acquired. As the Nazi party grew in Germany, so did the Hlinka party in Slovakia.

Hlinka's Slovak People's Party had been founded in 1913 by a Roman Catholic priest named Andrej Hlinka. The ideology of the party was both nationalistic and antisemitic. In the early years, the party idolized Slovak classical authors and religious leaders who were very clearly antisemitic. Some of these Slovak writers depicted the Jews as greedy, immoral and as leeches on Slovak society, bent on ruining the lives of the hardworking Slovak people. Often, they portrayed Jews as antisocial, with egotistical, domineering natures, much like Nazi propaganda did.

In the media, Jews were also accused of refusing to recognize the Slovaks as an equal nation to the Czechs and Hungarians. According to the articles, the Jews were power-hungry, always siding with the government in power to look down on the oppressed. Jews were especially portrayed as identifying with Hungarian or Czech culture rather than Slovak culture. They were considered enemies of the new state. Even some of the well-known songs of the time reflected a hatred for Jewish people. One song, the anthem of the Hlinka Guard, told of a Slovak fascist party visionary riding a train through the country, demonstrating the might of the party. The song used violent language, inciting hatred against the Jews by calling on the people to "cut and chop deep until blood flows."

Slovakia's new independence was overwhelming for most of the Slovak nation. Their statehood was unprecedented. As time passed, economic hardships began to affect the Jews more than the rest of the population. Due to new antisemitic laws, businesses were gradually taken away from us, schools closed their doors to Jewish students, and we were forbidden entrance to many public places.

By the time I was almost fifteen, I found myself out of school. Under normal circumstances I would have continued my studies in high school, but it was 1939, the year World War II began, and restrictions for Jews were increasing. The high school I would have attended was in a neighbouring town but three other things, not the distance, prevented me from going to the school: my mother needed me at home, we didn't have enough money for the cost of schooling, and by July 1939, quotas for Jews had been imposed (*numerus clausus*). Just over one year later, no Jews were allowed in secondary schools at all (*numerus nullus*). It wasn't until after the war, when I was married with four children, that I completed my high school education.

In the months following my interrupted schooling I continued to socialize with other young people my age or bit older, mostly former schoolmates. All the signs confirmed that our future was bleak. By the next year, in the fall of 1940, the restrictions were even more severe: Jews were not allowed to go to the markets, possess jewellery, own or use a radio, or own property. Step by step, our livelihoods were taken away. In September 1941, Slovakia enacted the Jewish Code, modelled on Germany's Nuremberg Laws, and we had to wear yellow armbands and yellow Stars of David displayed prominently on our clothing.

My nerves were on edge. Still, I tried to get the most out of life and occasionally I managed to get paid to do some chores, helping out in stores or neighbours' households. I ached to be creative, an urge that went unsatisfied. By now, many of my friends and I were drawn to Hashomer Hatzair, a Zionist youth group with a socialist ideology that we found more realistic and relevant to the world in which we now lived. We felt Zionism would help us survive. Never before did Hashomer Hatzair increase its membership more than in 1939. The organization promoted immigration to British Mandate Palestine and emphasized physical fitness and agricultural training that would later serve those who made it there to work the land.

All the Hashomer members I knew were highly educated and worldly, and I admired them greatly. Of course, they may have seemed that way to me because they were older. They knew how to explain things from different perspectives – historically, sociologically and economically. I found the atmosphere stimulating, and their discussions about the world around us insightful but not aggressive. We formed good working groups and developed lifelong friendships.

Some of our members left for Palestine at the last possible moment. I remained in contact only with those who stayed behind.

Sadly, I recall one of my many friends from the group, Ernie, who neither made it to Palestine nor even to the end of the war. Ernie was an ardent Zionist and a long-time Hashomer Hatzair member. He convinced many to go on the *hachshara* program, which trained young pioneers in leadership and education in preparation for their new and difficult life. Most of the *hachshara* participants eventually made aliyah – immigration to the Land of Israel – but Ernie never did. He left town with his father and, after the unsuccessful 1944 Slovak National Uprising against the fascists, he was found frozen to death in the woods.

$\sim$

During the idyllic, slow-paced years before the war, I became friends with a girl named Eva. It felt as though our friendship spanned all of our teenage years, yet now when I review those years, I am surprised to realize that we were actually friends for only three years.

I knew of Eva's family long before we became close. Her father was born in Humenné and had become a successful lawyer, known not only in our town, but far beyond it as well. Eva's mother was from somewhere in Hungary and her charm and refined manner further elevated the family's status. Eva used to say that her older brother inherited all of their parents' good looks because she felt that she got their less attractive features, but this was not entirely true. Eva had long, wavy, golden hair that caught everyone's attention. Her hair and nicely-shaped lips highlighted her face. Tall, confident and well-mannered, Eva walked the streets of our town doing her errands under the watchful eyes of her purebred German shepherd. I remember how she strolled along the streets with the dog always by her side.

Eva's family was one of the elite professionals of Humenné that I mentioned earlier who were quite isolated from the rest of the Jewish community. Her family's social circle was a small one, made up of a few close-knit Jewish and gentile families that were all wealthy and shared a privileged social status.

Eva was a good-natured girl and we were brought together by friends we had in common. I remember an occasion when Eva invited some of us to her home, a white villa at the intersection of two streets. The villa was large and took up a good portion of the corner. Behind the iron gates one could see the garden, lush with fruit trees. The villa itself had three entrances. We were never invited to see the house, aside from the very fancy kitchen and Eva's own room. That day, I, along with two other girls, spent the afternoon in her room, which was furnished with a white piano and a four-piece, white seating arrangement covered with embroidered upholstery. Her mother served us cocoa, homemade pastries and ice cream. We had a good time in these pleasant surroundings.

We were surprised when Eva's father entered the room to have a chat with us. He looked us over and wanted to know who we were and to whom we belonged. In short, he wondered about our social status. "I know you," said Eva's father to one of the girls. That particular girl's family also belonged to high society and, though the two families sometimes socialized, Eva's family was higher up on the social ladder. Eva's father seemed to approve of her presence. Then he turned to the second girl, Annie, and asked who she was. She said her name, adding proudly, "My father is a public notary. We moved to town only two years ago, so you might not know us." Eva's father thought this over before replying, "I know your parents perfectly well. I met them recently. Please enjoy your visit here." I was certain that Eva's father was only being polite and had never met her parents.

Now it was my turn. "And what is your name?" he asked me. I didn't want to say that my father wasn't born in the town. At any rate, Eva's father wouldn't have known him. We sold milk and dairy products to his household, but it would have been pointless to mention this; I was sure that purchasing food was not a part of his household routine. My mind went into high gear – I of course wanted to present my family in a positive light. I heard myself talking about my mother, who was born in Humenné. I told him her maiden name, thinking maybe he had heard of her – either because he too had been born in the town or because of her illness. Eva's father said, "You are Vilma Stern's daughter? She is well known for her cleanliness!" A weight lifted from my heart; I had been accepted! My mother's cleanliness had apparently opened the doors to "high society" for me. Or maybe Eva's father was simply being polite, as he had been to my other friend. Looking back on this episode now, I can see that the whole thing was petty, a scene that perhaps belonged to an earlier century.

〜

I have heard it said that Jews are united only in times when anti-semitism is raging. I find this sad, but in this case it was true. To the Nazis and Slovak antisemites, we were all evil Jews, the enemies of humankind. When it became clear that the fascists did not differentiate between socio-economic classes, prior class distinctions no longer really mattered. The lives we all knew were in the past.

Denunciations and, consequently, *razzias* – raids – on Jewish homes affected families like Eva's earlier than most. The Hlinka Guard targeted them right from the start. Rumour had it that her parents had been harassed and even physically attacked. Some felt that the fascists were especially hard on Eva's father because he was a lawyer. Their aim was to make life miserable for the Jews – especially those who had enjoyed wealth and privilege – and to steal their valuables for themselves.

Eva no longer walked proudly through the town with her handsome, beloved dog. One day, near the beginning of 1942, I opened the front door and found her standing there with a suitcase. She opened it and asked us to hide the contents – at least twenty pairs of brand new shoes. We agreed. On another day Eva came with a dozen or so tablecloths, and then again with other household goods. We put everything into my mother's armoire. No one from either of our families had the opportunity to ever use the hidden goods again.

The spring of 1942 heralded the most difficult time for Jews in our town. Humenné and its surrounding towns were among the first places in Slovakia to begin deportations to the death camps and the Slovak collaborators there became infamous for taking a leading role. The Nazis scheduled the first deportation for March 25, with transports of single women. Auschwitz and other camps in Poland were not yet household names – we could only guess where we would be taken. We wanted to believe the rumours that we would be brought to work making army boots in a shoe factory in Bat'ovany just two hours from Humenné.

Sometime in the middle of March, a week before the summons for the women's deportation, Eva and I discussed the situation of the upcoming transport. I told her that I hoped to be excused because of my mother's condition. Eva felt that her mother wouldn't survive her absence, but she didn't plan to hide because she feared that her parents would be killed for her disobedience.

I knew that I must not go with the women's transport. As an only child, I was certain that my parents wouldn't survive my deportation. Not only would they fear for my life, but my mother was also seriously ill with her congestive heart failure and my father and I alternated nursing her. My mother's role in my survival was a paradox. She often said, "I saved your lives," and for a time it seemed that this was indeed true. Caring for her was our priority and this had an impact on how we behaved and reacted to various situations. I suppose unusual circumstances create unusual responses.

When all the single women sixteen years and older were summoned to the police headquarters I reported along with them; however, unlike the others, I packed nothing. I was prepared to do whatever necessary to stay home with my mother. What naïveté! Only a few young women didn't report to the police – they went into hiding immediately.

In the vast courtyard of the police building, approximately 350 young women were assembled. I spent the whole day begging, crying and explaining my family's situation. I appealed to their hearts and consciences, asking for compassion, talking about human and Christian values, on and on from early morning until dusk. There was another woman there in a similar situation, also begging for pity.

At the end of the day the police figured out the total – the quotas had been filled. We were merely numbers to them, but to us each number represented a human life. Since we were not needed, they let me and the other woman go home. The other young women were deported that very night. It didn't take long for us to learn of their whereabouts. This first transport of single women from Slovakia went straight to Auschwitz. The women from Humenné were among the first Jewish *Häftlings*, inmates, there. Very few of them survived the war.

That day Eva had been among those who obeyed the summons, feeling she could do nothing else. I heard that the young women were lined up in columns of ten and when they were marched past Eva's house, her mother ran after her, knelt before a policeman and begged him to let her daughter go. He kicked her brutally and she fell into a coma. She passed away one week later. My friend Eva was one of Auschwitz's first victims.

Although at the time we didn't know the exact fate of the women, I sensed, as did many of us, the brutalities and hardships they would likely undergo. Not surprisingly, I suppose, I felt a painful emptiness. I was only seventeen years old and left in a town from which so many of my friends were taken.

It is hard to describe the deep relief with which my parents greeted me that evening when I was released. Our neighbours showed how happy they were for us by bringing flowers and fruit baskets. It was a remarkable conclusion to a horrific day. Imagine, two desperate young women begging for the lives of their parents as well as their own and unexpectedly given a reprieve when the situation appeared hopeless. I wonder if I was spared that time because my case was so very different from everyone else's or if it was simply a miracle. With each deportation, for those of us not taken, it felt as though a part of our souls perished along with the friends and families that were.

I relive that time over and over again. Even when dealing with practical matters, like when my father's birth certificate from Slovakia couldn't be located, it comes back to haunt me. Two world wars in one century ruined our part of the world in many ways; records of human lives were obliterated.

Searching for Safety

After that first transport of 1942, I periodically went into hiding to avoid the *razzias* aimed at Jewish homes. One day, when it was safe to be at home, I was approached by two of my friends from Hashomer Hatzair. They asked me to meet with one of their "cells." I had heard about these cells – they were often made up of four people and were a testing ground for young people who might be considered later on (once they had reached about eighteen years of age and proven their loyalty) to be part of a dangerous, but righteous cause – an underground resistance. This form of resistance was risky, especially since membership in any kind of socialist group was illegal at the time.

Without giving it much thought I agreed and was given a task – to go to a store on Masaryk Street that sold electrical supplies and collect a sum of money from the owner. I removed my yellow band and went to the shop, discreetly conveying my password to the shopkeeper behind the counter. I then asked him for a particular amount of money, as instructed. The owner of the store was the last man in our town whom I would have ever suspected of being part of the underground. Perhaps he thought the same about me. We knew each other, but beyond the script, we didn't say another word. He gave me the money and I took it and left.

My instructions were to purchase certain items of food with the money. I stopped in at a delicatessen and then a bakery, running into no difficulty at either place. In spite of all going smoothly, my heart was pounding wildly. What if I were caught? What if this was a trap? Who were these people to whom I must deliver the purchases? But the rule of the cell was never to ask questions, so I kept them to myself.

The final destination was a Greek Orthodox church located on Lipová, the street where I now lived. I had to ring twice in order to get a response. Finally the huge, iron gate was opened and I entered a courtyard. The main entrance was twenty steps further, but to me it felt like twenty kilometres. I gave two short rings, as I had been told, and the massive, wooden doors were opened. I gave my password and was told to leave the basket of food at the door and then to leave. I did so with great haste. When it was over I felt invigorated, as though I had accomplished something important and was part of a chain of actions that mattered. I never told my parents about this episode.

One week later I met up with the two friends who had recruited me and they thanked me for a job well done. It was then that I discovered how lucky I had been. The whole enterprise was betrayed the day after my task had been completed. The police raided the church and took those who were hiding inside to an unknown destination. No more cell sessions took place. My two friends were also lucky not to be caught. Soon after, they slipped away to hide and fight with the partisans in the Carpathian Mountains.

To tell what became of one of them, Jan, I have to skip ahead to September 1945. The war had been over for more than three months and I was living with my husband, Arthur, in Bratislava. In the course of our efforts to establish a new home, I had decided to return to Humenné to retrieve some articles belonging to my late father. At that time, the journey of approximately 450 kilometres took more than two days to travel by train, with a long stopover in the city of Košice. I passed the time by browsing along the streets, and by chance I met some old acquaintances. It was then that I learned of Jan's fate – he was in jail in Košice. He had been there for two months, awaiting a hearing. Jan had lost his whole family, fought the fascists as a partisan and survived the war only to sit in a Slovak jail. This information infuriated me and no logical reasoning could have stopped me as I went off in search of the prison to see my friend.

The story was that Jan had been accused of participating in the killing of a policeman while fighting in the Slovak National Uprising. While denying these allegations, he sat, frustrated, in jail. On impulse, I sought out the prosecutor and remarkably was granted an appointment in just one hour. I presented my case passionately, voice trembling, insisting that Jan had been falsely accused and must have a hearing at once. The prosecutor thought that my jailed friend and I were lovers; I assured him that our friendship was made of other stuff, born from the solidarity created by sharing a philosophy in desperate circumstances and a gruesome fate. I prayed that the prosecutor would believe me. My certainty of Jan's innocence must have been convincing. The prosecutor promised me that there would be a hearing the very next day.

By then, my train was due to depart in just thirty minutes. My feet barely touched the ground as I ran to the station, fuelled by the promise I had received – happily, a promise that was honoured. Jan was found innocent. He survived this last obstacle of the war and moved to Prague. We remain friends to this day.

$$\sim$$

During the horrific, eventful summer of 1942, we heard rumours that new transports would soon begin. My parents were understandably frightened by these reports and did not want me to stay at home. They couldn't hide because of my mother's illness and miraculously, for some reason, they weren't deported. Others in our town who were bedridden or in wheelchairs or otherwise disabled had already been deported, but she was not. Masaryk Street was busy now, filled with strangers in uniform. Whenever new faces appeared on the main street, it was a bad omen. By now we knew that organizers of the transports transferred members of the Hlinka Guard between cities because they were afraid that the local militia would be more sympathetic to the Jews than strangers.

During these months of unrest I hid in a variety of places, some that I cannot believe I managed to endure. These hiding spots were both my refuge and my private hell. It is an understatement to say that surviving such an ordeal deeply affected me. It was a waking nightmare.

One such abhorrent hiding place was a crawl space in another family's home, where I hid for about two weeks. I could do nothing but sit or lie in one position for hours on end. At night I could go out to attend to my personal hygiene and to stretch my muscles, but then I had to return to my prison. For about a week in the summer I also hid in an attic. It was unbearably hot – so much so that I fainted a few times. Still, each day in hiding was a day that I survived and was another day closer to the end of the war. Did I mention that I had been spoiled as a child? I was pampered no longer.

One of our old neighbours from Masaryk Street, Mrs. Rokov, who was very fond of our family, suggested that I come to stay in their wine cellar for a short time. Certainly no one would look for me there. The house was very old and solid, built of stone and bricks, and had withstood both natural and manmade catastrophes. The wine cellar, however, was everything I dreaded and despised. It was deep underground where it was damp, cold and dark and it didn't take me long to discover that I shared my quarters with a nest of mice. I dread rodents. Even now when I see a mouse, I shriek and jump up on a table or chair. In truth, I would even climb walls if I could, to avoid any kind of rodent. I cannot even look at a hamster. Even if a rodent is a remote image on television, I avert my eyes. It has been this way for me all my life, so imagine then, knowing my revulsion for these creatures, how insufferable it was. Yet, I had no choice but to hide in this rodent-infested place.

Although I was provided with food, a small round table, a comfortable chair and a dim light, the basement was nonetheless cold and frightening. Whenever I unlocked the door and turned on the light, I gave the mice time to disappear into their holes. Only then would I enter. Still, I felt their presence and heard them squeaking. Sometimes I saw mice running from one hole to another and I would try shining my flashlight at them to stop them from scurrying and squeaking. I think that mice must reproduce frequently. More times than I care to remember, I saw newborns, as many as ten mice in one litter. But, as miserable as it was, I had to consider myself lucky – I had no rats for roommates. I couldn't handle more than two or three days of this in a row, but I hid there on and off for about three weeks. It's no surprise that I developed a severe case of claustrophobia after this period of hiding.

Mrs. Rokov had known my mother for many years and felt sorry for her because of her illness. The Rokov family was wealthy and owned estates in the countryside near our town. They had two children – a daughter a few years older than me and a son who was younger. The Rokovs were traditional, conservative parents who brought up the children in a religious and conventional manner. Both children attended the town's only Catholic school. Before the war the couple had been completely apolitical – they focused on their family and business matters. As long as these were prospering, they didn't appear to care much about what was going on in the rest of the world.

As is often the case, in spite of their identical upbringing, the couple's children chose different directions in life. The daughter, essentially a good-natured girl, was less ambitious than her parents. She was introduced to a young man from a nearby village who had just recently finished law school. Both sets of parents approved of and encouraged this relationship and blessed their plans for the future.

As an ambitious young lawyer, however, the young man found it advantageous to enroll in the Hlinka party to secure a significant position. Although neither he nor his new wife had previously been particularly political, this was common in those days. Eventually the young couple moved to Bratislava, the capital, where better jobs were available. I lost track of them during the war, but met them again later in Bratislava.

Mrs. Rokov's son had gravitated to the youth group of the Hlinka party while still living with his parents. I don't know how his parents found the courage to hide me in their house while a member of their own family wore the black Guardists' uniform. I was even more afraid of the son, with his allegiance to the Hlinka party, than I was of the mice in the cellar. Fortunately, he had no taste for alcohol and so had no reason to go downstairs to the cellar. Much to his parents' chagrin, his interests lay completely outside of the house and he was seldom at home.

My parents, of course, felt deep gratitude toward the family and included them in their prayers. These people placed themselves in a position of great danger for us. Neither the daughter nor the son was aware of my hiding in their cellar – their parents had to be very cautious. To be discovered helping a Jew would have earned them the label of "White Jew." Not only would it have damaged their reputation, but it also could have jeopardized their safety.

~

In July 1942, my aunt Dorothy, her husband, Emil, and their two small children, Erwin and Kati, were deported from Humenné to Auschwitz. I had nightmares about them for many years after, often waking from sleep sweating and gasping for air, with my heart beating wildly. These disturbing dreams left me weak and trembling.

At the height of the deportations my aunt had come to us, asking for my parents to take her family in. For quite a long time I struggled with the implications of the horrible decision my father had to make – a decision to protect the lives of his wife and daughter before that of his sister and her family. Although it wasn't my decision to make, in dreams I was haunted by my conscience, overwhelmed both in body and soul. I couldn't understand my aunt at the time. We were as vulnerable as they were. We were all in the same boat, all in danger of sinking. How could one innocent person who was condemned to death help to save the life of another innocent person condemned to the same fate?

We were living on Lipová Street, where we had moved in 1934, and there was no place to hide in our small apartment. We were all living in one room now, with an adjoining bathroom and a kitchen. We were three adults, one constantly sick and in bed. How could my aunt ask such a helpless family for shelter? To this day, I periodically analyze it. Is my conscience not yet clear?

In my dreams about their family, baby Erwin appeared taller than other children his age. He was just three years old and always well-dressed in a crisp, white shirt and shiny, black shoes. His brown hair was wavy, making him look almost girlish. But in my nightmares Erwin didn't like girls – actually, he was not fond of other children at all. My mind depicted Erwin playing alone with a doll that had blue eyes and brown hair like his while the other boys made fun of him. In these dreams I was one of his teachers. On walks in the woods with the children it was as if Erwin became a different child. He jumped, laughed and ran from us, deep into the forest. I was always searching for Erwin in those dreams. Sometimes I felt so frustrated when he disappeared; I would run after him, but could never find him. I ran deeper and deeper into the woods but Erwin was nowhere to be found. It was as if he had vanished. In one dream I ran until I fell on little prickly bushes. Finally, bleeding and sweating, someone, I don't know who, helped me to my feet. When we returned to the playground there sat Erwin, playing quietly with his doll.

In reality, there was little opportunity in Erwin's short life for me to look after him or his younger sister, Kati, who was one year old when I last saw her. She had blue eyes just like my aunt's. Sometimes in my dreams I saw Kati walking with my aunt. She was a happy little girl, holding her mother's hand. I studied her carefully, wanting to know her, and I would call out to them loudly, crying as I called their names with all my might. But they could never hear me. I wanted to run to them, but something in the grass always hindered my efforts. In one dream my parents visited the playground I had created in my mind. We all sat playing with the school children in the fresh air when suddenly my aunt and uncle, with the two children, started moving slowly toward us, dressed in the same summer outfits I remember seeing them in last. Sometimes in my dreams my cousins grew very quickly before my eyes. "Stop!" I cried out. "Enough! Don't grow anymore!" I was afraid that if they grew too tall they would obstruct my view and take the light from me.

I understood that to have provided them with shelter would have jeopardized our own precarious situation, and I think my aunt was wrong to have asked my father for a place to hide. My father was a devoted brother, husband and father and under most circumstances he would have offered to help anyone he could. In this case, he felt he had no choice. My aunt was not thinking clearly. In desperation she had asked her brother to risk his family's safety and he, equally desperate, had to refuse. At the time, I had many arguments in my mind as to what was right.

Eventually, my dream encounters with baby Erwin and Kati became more peaceful. My nightmares were a part of how I dealt with surviving my loved ones' deaths. It would seem that now I have also survived my nightmares.

~

During the rest of that summer of 1942 the Slovak state continued to fill the Nazis' deportation quotas and we never knew when we could expect an unwelcome and dreaded visit from the Hlinka Guard. By then the Jewish community was organized. We considered our representatives – members of the Jewish council, or Judenrat – to be like a bridge, separating us from the enemy, but also serving as a connection for the executioners. I think that the Jewish council representatives tried their best to extend their limited powers. Often their own families benefited the most, but at least we had somewhere to turn when needed.

More than ever, money "talked" in those days. Money was an important factor – you could buy your life with it if you knew the right people. People who could afford it paid for their lives with cash, properties or other valuables. They gave everything to save their most valuable possession of all – their families. My family didn't have money or affluent connections so we had nothing to use to save our lives.

Some well-to-do Jews had acquired valuable presidential exemptions, which protected them from deportation. The state issued these exemptions to Jews who were acknowledged as economically important to the country by virtue of their profession or the business they owned. Once Jews were no longer allowed to own their own businesses, Aryan Slovaks known as *arizátors* came forward to assume at least half of the ownership. In most cases, the *arizátors* eventually began to manage the businesses on their own, and when they no longer required help from the former Jewish owners, the presidential exemptions had dubious value.

Some institutions of the state attempted to protect us. The Slovak state was led by Roman Catholics, who held all of the political and economic advantages, whereas the Lutherans, Protestants and Greek Orthodox were powerless. The members of these latter denominations were understandably unhappy to be so far removed from the centre of power. As a result, they demonstrated (more or less silently) a moderate amount of sympathy and understanding toward the Jews. Many members of the clergy did what they could by issuing conversion certificates. Our local Greek Orthodox religious leader was one of those who helped, although many believed that he acted out of hatred for the religion in power, Catholicism, or for money. Nonetheless, we felt that many other religious leaders acted primarily out of compassion for us. They persevered in these efforts, even though it soon became clear that while the Christian community was trying to protect some of us by issuing conversion certificates, the Jewish Code then in force defined Jews by their ancestry as far as four generations back. In the end, the conversion certificates were of little benefit.

My father was one of those who received a certificate of conversion to Greek Orthodoxy and was given the typical Russian middle name of Vasilij. He was now Samuel Vasilij Weinberger, a very bizarre combination of names. We hoped that he wouldn't find himself in a situation where he would be required to produce the certificate. But in August 1942, five months after the transport of single women, such a situation did, in fact, arise.

A great deal had happened in those five months and we grew wiser from day to day, gaining knowledge with each new experience. By then the intentions of our enemies were crystal-clear and so was our fate. With the deportations of single women, single men and then whole families, the Jewish population in our town had visibly dwindled.

We had learned through rumours that a labour camp had been established in Ilava, the northwest region of Slovakia, for men and women of mixed marriages or for those who had converted. There had been no deportations from there so far. Rather than wait to be taken in a *razzia* or a deportation, my father enlisted for forced labour and was due to depart in two weeks.

I had already begun my episodes of hiding, but at that time, I was home for a few days, as it seemed that there were no deportations in the air. Early on that warm August morning when we almost lost my father, I lay sleeping on a sofa next to the open windows of our main floor apartment. Suddenly, I heard someone calling my name. "Zuzana! Zuzana! Wake up! Hurry! Get up!" Opening my eyes, I looked outside and saw Jozef, a man I knew from the Roma community (we called them Gypsies at the time), who had worked in our previous neighbourhood. Although my family had moved to our present apartment eight years earlier and I didn't recall seeing Jozef in that time, he obviously knew how to locate us.

The Roma of Humenné lived in a small group of inexpensive houses outside of the town. A handful of Roma worked in the town, mainly helping shopkeepers with heavy, manual labour. Jozef was one of them. I specifically remembered him from my childhood when we had lived on Masaryk Street. Most of the children, including me, were afraid of the Roma. Although they were not threatening to us in any way, they were social outcasts and many people in our town considered them to be disreputable. To the outside observer, the Roma appeared to always be on the move. They were stereotyped as untrustworthy. During the war, the "Gypsy Question" was close to the top of the Nazi agenda, just below the "Jewish Question," and they were also being heavily persecuted.

Jozef told me that at six o'clock that morning he had seen a policeman leading my father and others out of the *shtiebl*, the small synagogue, or prayer house. Jozef had followed them to police headquarters and, realizing the seriousness of the situation, ran to inform us. When Jozef arrived at our apartment to alert us, it was just six-thirty in the morning.

I wondered if anyone other than Jozef had witnessed my father being taken away by the police. For God's sake, I wondered, why was he so eager to go to synagogue? He could have prayed at home. But I knew my father. He wanted to be a part of the minyan – the quorum required for certain prayers – instead of saying his morning prayers at home alone. The synagogue we belonged to had been closed for half a year – there were no longer enough people to fill it. When my father was apprehended in the *shtiebl*, only a small group of Jews remained to form the minyan.

Before these tragic times, Jewish life in Humenné was vibrant and had three places of worship. The Orthodox synagogue where my father had worshipped was the most widely attended, with an impressive new building that had been constructed in the early 1930s. Long before the war, when the Jewish community was thriving, the synagogue had commemorated all of the Czechoslovak national holidays and invited local dignitaries, including the mayor and even the colonel of the local military squadron, on significant national occasions.

When Jozef advised me of what had happened, I dressed quickly, asked him to stay with my anxious mother and ran looking for the Jewish Council representatives, hoping for assistance. I located one man whom I knew fairly well, but he was very discouraging. He told me that a transport was due again and the police needed to fill a quota of one hundred people by that evening. He concluded that it was pointless to go after my father. I left for the police headquarters alone.

I arrived at the headquarters at seven a.m. The building was still, as if in a deep sleep. The main office would not be open for another hour. I searched through the few hallways and finally found the officer on call, a man who was not familiar to me. His face was expressionless and he appeared to be totally disinterested in me or my dilemma. I urged him to release my father so that he might go home to his sick wife. I could not have pleaded more passionately if I had been down on my knees. I heard myself claiming that he had been taken mistakenly, that he was a Christian and his presence at the synagogue was a mistake. I promised it would never happen again. The policeman looked closely at the clock hanging on the wall. By this time it was seven fifteen. Without saying a word he left the office and with his finger indicated that I should follow him. I waited outside the office on the stairs.

When I finally saw my father almost half an hour later, he looked shattered, still clutching his navy-blue velvet bag that held his prayer book, *tallis* – prayer shawl – and *tefillin* – phylacteries. In my father's pocket was the certificate of conversion. The officer made no comment about the bag, or its contents, and paid no attention to my expressions of gratitude either. Maybe his thoughts were elsewhere, or maybe he was nervous. Lucky for us, he didn't seem particularly dedicated to the requirements of his job. I only wish that more officials in his position had behaved similarly. Eventually, he said, "Go. And go fast!"

On the way home my father and I held hands tightly as we silently approached our apartment. We arrived to find Jozef still there, waiting, with my mother. They stared at us, unable to believe their eyes.

When I re-examine this event, and the many others associated with my eventual survival, I wonder what force pushed me. What prompted me to go to the police headquarters? Did I lack the instinct for self-preservation? Maybe I wasn't smart enough to see the danger I was in. Maybe, like most young people, I overestimated my invincibility. I could barely endure the places in which I was forced to hide, yet when my father was taken, I threw myself into the lion's den! Perhaps I would have been more afraid if members of the paramilitary Hlinka Guard had been involved – not all the police were necessarily members of the fascist party.

At any rate, I suppose it's easy to see that my decision that morning wasn't a rational one. I was simply a young, loving daughter, determined that her father not be taken away from his family. I had begged once before and it worked, so I simply tried the same tactic again. I had an overwhelming feeling that to let my father perish would mean our demise as well. It was a stroke of luck that this all occurred before the police department office opened at eight a.m. so that no one else witnessed the officer allowing my father to leave. Half an hour or so later, the offices would have been full of people beginning their daily work.

The others incarcerated in the basement of police headquarters that morning were deported. I was eternally grateful to Jozef. If not for him, the news of my father's arrest wouldn't have reached me in time. "Oh, God," I thought, after the incident was over, "you have been so good to us so far! Please keep watching over us."

Escape to Hungary

I had been in hiding on and off for more than a year when my mother passed away, succumbing to her illness on July 23, 1943. My father was in Ilava, the labour camp reserved for those with certificates of conversion. It was a place considered to be safer than the other camps, and he was even allowed a short leave once a month. Unfortunately, he did not make it back in time for the funeral, but he arrived two days later and we sat shiva together.

Following my mother's death, I became seriously ill with scarlet fever, which was then a highly contagious and often deadly disease. I was kept in isolation in the hospital for two months, too sick to care about the war or even events just outside the hospital walls. The nurses were nuns who merely went about their business. I had no visitors while I was in the hospital – people generally only visit hospitals during times of peace. At any rate, most of my friends were either in hiding, suffering the horrors of the camps, or they were already dead. I don't think anyone even knew of my whereabouts. Under the circumstances, it was difficult to keep track of anyone.

Shortly after my bout with scarlet fever, I fell sick again and was admitted to the hospital once more – this time with a severe case of jaundice – and was there for another month. Up until that time, I had never suffered from any serious illness, but these admissions to the hospital turned out to be the safest periods I could have had.

Ironically, my illnesses protected me for three precious months. I was spared from hiding in unsavoury conditions and evaded deportation as well.

By the end of 1943, five months after my mother's passing, I felt it was time for me to flee the country. Although there had been some periods of relative calm when there weren't any deportations, I knew I could no longer stay in Humenné alone. Soon after I was discharged from the hospital, I met the man who would become my husband, Arthur Sermer. He, his brother Victor and their cousin Leah were staying with their aunt, who happened to be my neighbour. We all agreed that remaining in Slovakia was too dangerous. All of my hiding places had been exhausted and Arthur was being hunted by the Gestapo because they knew he had been in touch with partisans on the Polish border. We decided to seek refuge in Hungary. Arthur had a contact who led us to a series of further contacts who eventually produced a smuggler who, for a sum of money, would get us across the border.

～

Arthur's family came from Nižné Zbojné, a village surrounded by hilly forests on the edge of the Carpathian Mountains, some twenty kilometres north of Humenné. The land they owned yielded harvests of wheat, rye, barley, corn and potatoes. For the most part, Arthur's family managed the work themselves, hiring additional labour from the village when required.

This was, of course, before the marvels of farm machinery had made its way to that part of the world. Crops were first and foremost for the family's own consumption – any excess was then sold. Arthur's family also raised some cattle, which grazed in the open fields, and they had chicken coops and a barn with ducks and geese.

Although it was a productive farm, farming was not as lucrative as it may have appeared. To supplement their income, the family also ran a general store. This was a welcome convenience for the villagers since it saved them the longer journey to the large neighbouring towns and cities for their various household needs. Arthur's oldest sister, Cecilia, managed the store. The income from the store would be a major source of her dowry. His other three sisters, Sophia, Anna and Sidonia, helped out as well.

Arthur's family observed Jewish tradition and his father was knowledgeable in Jewish teachings and law, so much so that Jews from many of the surrounding villages came to seek his advice. When they each turned four years old, Arthur and his brothers, Victor and Eman, were taught by their father as well. They rose earlier than the rest of the family and stayed up late to learn. They worked so hard and kept such long hours that sometimes father and sons dozed off in the middle of their lessons. When they were older, a Hebrew teacher who moved into the area took over the boys' Jewish education.

As the children grew, Arthur's parents wanted them to pursue further studies, but the closest schools were in Humenné. His father decided to build a schoolhouse in town to accommodate the village children and reduce the costs that would have resulted from travelling back and forth. The schoolhouse was also meant to be an investment. Unfortunately, this was in the aftermath of the Great Depression and the builder faced some serious problems. He went bankrupt before the project was completed. The whole family pitched in, working very hard and making many sacrifices to ensure that the schoolhouse was indeed finished.

By the time the years of peril and tragedy began for the Jews, most of Arthur's siblings had grown up, completed their education and no longer lived at home. Only the youngest two children, Sidonia and Victor, remained at home with their parents. But when the deportation of Jews to concentration camps began in Slovakia, most of the family came home to be with their parents. They chose to resist together and, along with other Jews from local villages, they decided to escape into the forests and hide. They began to prepare by collecting and storing food and supplies. The people knew the area well, so the forest was a natural hiding place. A huge tent, hidden deep in the woods, became home to thirty people of various ages – men, women, boys and girls. The group moved into the woods toward the middle of May 1942. They gladly endured the inconvenience of life in the woods, all in the one tent, but it was to be short-lived. The hiding place extended their lives by only about six weeks.

Shortly before the end of June, the group learned that they had been betrayed. They were beginning to pack up to flee when suddenly the Slovak gendarmes arrived. A few shots were fired into the air and the police, using loudspeakers, demanded their surrender. In a panic, the unarmed people began to run in all directions. Twenty-three were captured and taken to the nearest railway station, where a transport train awaited them.

Among the seven who were able to escape deeper into the forest were Arthur and Victor. At the time, Arthur was thirty and Victor was eighteen. They found the other members of the group and began to search for a new hiding place. They stayed in the forest for just over a year, but eventually the situation became intolerable and members of the group separated. It was not long after that I met Arthur, Victor and their cousin Leah, and we began to plan our escape to Hungary.

~

It was a bitterly cold, starless January night in 1944 when we left Slovakia, illegally crossing the border into Hungary. The air trembled in anticipation of a blizzard and only the white, glowing snow lit our way. We rode in a carriage pulled by a single horse, led by a smuggler who was profiting greatly from these midnight journeys.

Compared to Slovakia, which was eager to cooperate in Hitler's "Final Solution" – finishing off all the Jews as quickly and inexpensively as possible – Hungary appeared relatively safe at this time. Hungary, too, was considered an independent state, although it was politically allied with the Axis. The price for the country's so-called independence from Germany was to live by the Nazis' rules. All restrictions concerning the Jews, such as those dictating employment, schooling and property expropriation, were similar to those in other occupied European countries. Jews who were eligible for military service were assigned to labour camps, but this was preferable to the deportations in Slovakia, which led to the death camps in Poland.

In January 1944, Hungary was still home to more than 700,000 Jews. Thus far, the government had resisted sending its Jewish citizens to their deaths at Auschwitz and, influenced by this common knowledge, we embarked on our journey. The smuggler left us when we reached the border town of Sátoraljaújhely, at which point we travelled by train to Budapest. This leg of the trek was, fortunately, uneventful.

Before the war, I had often spent summer vacations in Budapest with my cousins and I looked forward to seeing my relatives again. Being a girl from a small town, I admired Budapest's beauty and considered it quite a grand city, with its well-tended gardens and baroque palaces situated on wide boulevards along the shores of the Danube River. My relatives on my father's side lived quite close to the Eastern Railway Station, where my travel companions and I disembarked. Leah left our group to stay with friends, and Arthur and Victor would stay elsewhere as well, but I led the way to my aunt Ethel's home to introduce them. I was very excited – my heart was pounding, synchronized with the pace of my steps. When we arrived in Budapest, I was nineteen years old. Aunt Ethel's sons were close to me in age; my cousin Feri was twenty and cousin Jozsi was eighteen. It was good to be with family once again.

Before long, I owned a false ID under the Polish Catholic name of Helena Smutek, which my cousins had acquired from some Polish Jews. Suddenly my life became busy and full. Feri knew I had studied many languages – German, Polish, Russian and French – and encouraged me to continue to study. He paid for me to study French with a man named Professor Homed, who was close to the family. The professor came to our home four times each week, tutoring my cousins and some of their friends in languages they normally would have been studying at school. The Jewish *gimnázium,* high school, had been closed, leaving many young people desperate to continue their studies rather than lose years of schooling.

How my relatives got to know Mr. Homed is a mystery to me. They had a very cordial relationship with him and he was paid handsomely for his lessons. It wasn't until many years after the war that my cousin Jozsi told me that his father, my uncle Andor, was not as comfortable with Homed as he seemed to be and referred to him as "the snake." Nonetheless, the teacher often joined the family at the table for lunch and sometimes for dinner as well. Silently, I marvelled at the way my aunt managed to stretch the food rations. The amount was not even sufficient for her own family.

As far as we knew, Mr. Homed was a refugee from Vienna. My relatives had no reason to question his background. His private life was never discussed, as members of my family were not in the habit of poking their noses into other people's business. But in March 1944, Mr. Homed played a significant role in our family – one that would bring my two-month period of relative safety to an end.

At this point, Hungary was trying to get out of the war and their alliance with Germany. The Nazis were displeased with these intentions and were especially irritated that the Hungarian government continued to resist deporting its Jews to death camps in Poland. Not surprisingly, yet somehow still shocking to us, the German army marched into Hungary on March 19, 1944, accompanied by the Gestapo and SS. They brought with them Nazi intolerance and new, barbaric laws. The Gestapo officers were especially bloodthirsty and keen to replenish their bottomless coffers to satisfy their growing taste for luxury items. The situation worsened for the many who had fled neighbouring states to seek asylum in Hungary, as there were frequent *razzias* – or roundups – on the streets and in homes. Spying and denunciations were also on the rise.

Hungary was now a land occupied by foreign military and political forces. The situation grew worse day by day, especially for the Jews. It was not wise to underestimate the SS and the Gestapo, or the power of Hungary's fascist Arrow Cross Party and the country's gendarmes. The Arrow Cross, or Nyilas, was akin to a Hungarian Gestapo. A highly nationalistic, antisemitic party, they had been banned in Hungary until the Nazis invaded and legalized their brand of terror against the Jews.

As this was happening, I continued living with my relatives and studying with Mr. Homed. Feri's friends often gathered in our home. In the course of these meetings, I learned that approximately twenty of them had been summoned to labour camps. This was the way Hungarian Jews fulfilled their military service. Feri wasn't summoned because of his long history of rheumatic heart disease, which had afflicted him throughout his life. Although his body was frail, Feri's mind was not, and he was a natural leader.

All of these young people were horrified at the thought of serving in the forced labour camps and they were looking for other alternatives. At this opportune time, Mr. Homed also suggested that they not go to the labour camps. "Escape!" he said, "Be part of the partisan fight under Tito. Go to Tito!" Mr. Homed assured the young men that if they gave him time, he would find a way to get them to Josip Tito, the leader of the Yugoslav partisans. They put their fate in his hands.

Two weeks passed and the date of the summons was rapidly approaching. We were all kept in suspense, waiting for Mr. Homed's plan to materialize. The boys readied themselves to go at a moment's notice, while their parents tried to prepare themselves emotionally. No one rushed Mr. Homed; he was, after all, their only hope. He was highly respected and all of the families had faith in him.

One week before the date of the summons, in mid-April 1944, Mr. Homed triumphantly proclaimed that he had found reliable contacts to get the boys to Tito's partisans. We could all feel the excitement. Mr. Homed was going to help save our young men! The group of twenty boys were to meet at ten o'clock sharp the next Monday morning, to the left of the main entranceway of the Southern Railway Station, in front of the deli.

The day before that fateful Monday, we saw Mr. Homed for the last time. When Monday morning came, the families said their goodbyes at home, knowing that it would be risky to arrive en masse at the station. Only Thomas, the fifteen-year-old brother of one boy in the group, went along to watch from a safe distance. Suddenly, he noticed men in uniform suspiciously close to where our young men had gathered. He searched desperately for his brother among the others and ran to him. His brother gave Thomas a piece of paper and said, "Give this to Feri." On the paper he had written, "The trip is treif [not kosher]. Our plan was betrayed." We found out later that the group was deported and eventually taken to camps in Poland.

Thomas took the note from his brother at eleven a.m. At five o'clock that same afternoon sirens roared throughout Budapest and planes from the Bacska region filled the sky. We ran to a shelter where we sat, barely speaking, overwhelmed and devastated from the morning's shocking events. It was clear that Feri had to get away quickly. None of us could imagine life without him, but if he didn't leave soon, he too would certainly be deported by the Germans. We all agreed that Feri should leave the next day and stay with a cousin living on the outskirts of Pest. My relatives thought that he would be okay for the next twenty-four hours. But they underestimated the Germans.

That night, Aunt Hannah and I went to sleep in the room we shared. In our queen-size bed, we tucked the blankets under our chins, shivering from the horrible chill we felt, made even worse by the cold draft in our poorly heated apartment. At two a.m. a noise from the adjacent room disturbed our sleep and a moment later, two uniformed men entered our bedroom. In German, my aunt was asked for her ID, a request that was then translated into Hungarian. Hannah put on her dressing gown and presented her ID. It passed inspection. When the police asked for my ID, Hannah told them I was only a child and, as the light was dimmed, they believed her; for some reason, they didn't bother to check. Her quick thinking may have saved my life, for my false papers were no guarantee of safety. Feri, however, was not so lucky. He was taken by the Gestapo, who suspected him of being a political opponent because of a Masaryk medal he kept, which, coincidentally, I had given to him many years before. He was deported to the Dachau concentration camp, but managed to survive there.

After the tragic events of that unforgettable night, I had to leave my aunt's home. Arthur, Victor and I knew that our brief time of refuge in Hungary was coming to an end. We began looking for a contact to smuggle us back to Slovakia and knew of others with similar intentions. In the meantime, we found a place to stay – a large apartment that was known to many refugees. The landlord allowed it to be used as a meeting place.

One day at dawn, the apartment was raided by the local police. Our IDs did not satisfy them – saying they had more questions, they whisked us off to the state security police headquarters in the Buda-Svábhegy district. Here, we experienced first-hand the work of professional interrogators.

I delivered my prepared story, maintaining that I was of Polish-Catholic descent. I explained why I spoke Hungarian by claiming that although my father was Polish, from Krakow, my mother had been Hungarian. In the past, Hungary and Poland had had a strong alliance. Because of this friendship, Hungary had unofficially offered shelter to members of the Polish army, defectors from the front. There were non-Jewish civilians from Poland who took refuge in Hungary as well. These circumstances made it plausible for Jews from Poland and other places to use false IDs and try to save their lives in Hungary by hiding their real identity.

I proved to be an easy subject for the interrogators. At nineteen years of age I was not prepared to handle such a situation. I recited my story in Hungarian, but they did not believe me. When I denied the allegation that I was Jewish, the detectives became infuriated and they began to beat my hands. My palms swelled instantly; second-by-second the flesh rose like yeast dough. I couldn't move my fingers, but the interrogator had no difficulty moving his. He pulled out my hair in clumps. I remember clearly how my hair stuck to the palms of his hands.

Ultimately they got out of me what they wanted to hear – that I was Jewish. This meant, of course, that Arthur, who had become my fiancé soon after we arrived in Budapest, and his brother were also Jewish. I learned later that they were both beaten much more severely than I was.

Now that they had established that we were Jewish, they knew what to do with us. We were taken with many others to a newly created transit camp in an old abandoned school located in the middle of Pest. There were hundreds of people already gathered there from all around Budapest. As of yet, no Jewish organization knew of the existence of this camp. It was horrific. There was no place to sleep, scarcely any food and no facilities for personal hygiene. Among the prisoners were families with small children. We were imprisoned there for two or three weeks.

Our next destination was Csepel, an island on the Danube that mainly housed the Manfred Weiss Works, a well-known armaments and industrial factory owned by Manfred Weiss, a Hungarian Jew, and three other interrelated families. Weiss and his family had, by now, fled Hungary after bartering their shares in the factory in exchange for their lives. The factory, the biggest in the country, manufactured a variety of products, including motorcycles, dishes and ammunition. Each product was manufactured in a separate building. Now under control of the SS, some of the factory was still operational and was being used to produce items for military purposes. The building we were taken to, however, served as the premises for yet another newly created transit camp. We learned that, again, our stay here would only be temporary.

Three weeks later we were moved once more. This time we were taken to a derelict brick factory located on the banks of the Danube in the town of Békásmegyer, on the edge of Budapest. We learned very quickly that people were being deported from the brick factory to Poland. By now, we knew exactly what awaited us in Poland.

The factory, connected to a working railway, was surrounded by SS officers. Freight trains stood close by, waiting to be filled. There were no passenger cars on these freight trains – only large cattle cars. We overheard from the Hungarian gendarmes that 30,000 people were incarcerated at this factory, ranging from newborns to the elderly. Typhoid fever and dysentery spread rapidly and the sick lay on bricks in the open yard of the factory.

The three of us found an area where we could move some bricks around in order to make a place to sit and to sleep. At night I awoke to feel raindrops washing over my face. This rainwater would be my only drink for the day. Conditions here were difficult, to say the least, but as a young person I found it possible to cope. For some of the older people, I think it was the beginning of the end. I recognized a distant, older relative of mine on my mother's side, Bella, from Humenné – it was extremely disturbing to see her in such a place. I remember being much more distressed by her discomfort than by my own. The brick factory was the last place I saw her.

Arthur was our leader, both spiritually and practically. At thirty-two he was older and more experienced than Victor, who was twenty-one, and I, two years younger still. Arthur vowed that we would not leave the brick factory in a cattle car. Having escaped from his village to the forests of Slovakia, Arthur had learned a great deal and had survived numerous police attacks. We relied on him to get us through this.

One day we witnessed a tall man, a Polish Jew in his thirties with blue eyes, blond hair and a fair complexion, standing in front of an SS official. With an irate voice the SS officer ordered the man to turn from side to side. Then he taunted him saying, "You may not be Jewish, but your nose certainly is!" We learned that this man and his

Polish friends were trying to get out of the camp by maintaining that they were Polish gentiles who had been rounded up in a street *razzia* and brought to the brick factory by mistake.

The three of us had now been imprisoned for almost two months and had no access to world news. But the determination and desperation of the Poles to use any means to get out of the brick factory and evade the awaiting cattle cars made an impression on us. We gathered that something new was going on out there.

It was the now the end of June 1944, and by talking to the Poles we learned that the Hungarian government was under international pressure to halt the deportations. This meant a slightly better situation for the Jews. Although this was good news, we all realized that the Germans would not allow Hungary to yield to the pressure. Among the captives there, the Polish Jews were the most well-informed and sensitive to danger. They knew how to evaluate and weigh our situation. If they felt this was the time to find a way out, then so should we.

Arthur insisted that we too maintain that we were rounded up mistakenly. At first I was vehemently opposed to this plan and I fought with Arthur about it. My interrogation at the police headquarters was still fresh in my mind. I vividly recalled the horrible hours I spent there and dreaded the thought of falling into their hands again. It was difficult to overcome my fears, but eventually I grew weary of arguing. In the end, fortunately, I went along with him, although needless to say I was frightened.

We lined up with many Poles to plead our case. Fortunately, we were not dealing with an SS official, as had the Polish Jew, but with Hungarian officers. Perhaps there had been new instructions from the top, for when we continued to claim that we had Polish backgrounds, that we were captured mistakenly and that we wanted to have a hearing, the Hungarians responded positively. They also appeared to believe the thirty other people who had very similar stories. We noticed a group of SS officers standing off to the side, eyeing us with hatred. In German we heard them complain, "This is their flight!" by which they meant that we were going to get away.

Thirty thousand people were imprisoned in the abandoned brick factory, Jews of all ages, from all walks of life – some sick, some strong, all on their way to die in the gas chambers of Auschwitz. For some reason, out of 30,000 people only thirty, all Polish Jews except for the three of us, found the courage to go to the authorities and assert that they didn't belong there. Of course, the Hungarian Jews couldn't have used the same story that we did. We were foreigners – which was noticeable by our accent – and we used that to our advantage. It was clear that we wouldn't be freed, but by being taken for further investigation we hoped to avoid the fate of those who were taken away in the cattle cars.

The Hungarian policemen then took us to one of Budapest's biggest prisons, Toloncház. The prison was full of criminals, but we didn't complain. What mattered was that there weren't any deportations from there. People mistakenly caught in *razzias*, as a rule, remained in prison until the authorities reached a further decision. The police didn't believe that thirty people could simply talk their way out of the hands of the SS and their Hungarian collaborators, so they were convinced that our group certainly couldn't be Jewish. Still, they didn't know what to make of us. We may not have been Jews, and we didn't appear to be criminals either. While they were puzzling over us, we happily settled in, hoping to wait out the war in these much more bearable surroundings, where we felt relatively safe.

If I had been alone, I would not have dared to plead my case at the brick factory. Undoubtedly, I would have ended up in the cattle cars. Again, it was as if a mighty force was behind me that pointed my steps, and those of Arthur and Victor, in the right direction – toward life.

Another Close Call

We had been in Toloncház for almost a month when we were informed that over the course of the next two days we would all be moved to a labour camp in Sátoraljaújhely north of Budapest and close to the border of Slovakia. We had hoped to be able to remain in prison until the end of the war, since this afforded us somewhat more safety and comfort than the obvious alternatives. I remember the conditions in Toloncház very clearly and how preferable they were to the transit camps. By wartime standards, we lived in the lap of luxury – after all, we ate three meals a day. Who cared that the meal consisted of a warm brown liquid with some half-cooked barley accompanied by a stale piece of bread?

We lived and slept in a huge hall along with approximately one hundred other prisoners who, like us, awaited decisions regarding their fates. There were mattresses filled either with straw or rags to sleep on. Unlike typical prison inmates, men and women were placed together, and we were free to walk about the hall and interact with each other.

When we heard the news that our departure was imminent, I took out my small supply of hydrogen peroxide – among the few possessions I had carried with me from one internment to another – and began to re-dye my hair. From the time the Germans had marched into Slovakia, I had been bleaching my hair to appear more Aryan. A

hairdresser in Humenné had spent a great deal of time – and peroxide
– transforming my dark brown locks to blond. Obviously I couldn't
afford to have my new look maintained by a professional, but I did
my best with a few bottles of peroxide, using it sparingly to touch up
my roots. There was a bonus in using peroxide at Tolonchház – it was
also effective in killing lice, one of prison life's gifts.

Near the end of July 1944, our next destination was the labour
camp in Sátoraljaújhely, the same town we had passed through on
our original escape into Hungary. Under the Austro-Hungarian Empire, Sátoraljaújhely had been considered an important commercial
centre, sitting on the crossroads between the Baltic Sea and the Mediterranean. After World War I the town's importance diminished and
it became a relatively insignificant border town.

The prisoners at the labour camp in Sátoraljaújhely were a very
different combination of people from those we had seen previously.
Here we were among non-Jewish refugees from the Ukraine, Belarus
and Poland, many of whom had brought along sheep, cows and other
domestic animals when they were fleeing the rapidly advancing Soviet army. Our groups did not mix. We watched each other somewhat
suspiciously from a distance. As far as we were concerned, if these
people were running from the Soviets and along with the German
army, they must have been collaborators involved in local politics and
perhaps even atrocities.

Our fellow prisoners knew who we were. We expected to be exposed and, as it turned out, we did not have long to wait. Shortly after
our arrival, we were told to remain in our rooms. Rumour had it that
the authorities were planning physical examinations of the men. In
Europe at the time, only Jews circumcised their newborn sons, so
circumcision was sufficient proof of a man's Jewish identity. After the
war, many Jewish mothers were reluctant to continue this tradition –
history had taught us to think about our children's safety.

As women, we felt lucky to avoid the physical exams, but one of
my fellow Jewish inmates made it clear that no one was safe from

the Germans. She had once witnessed a scene where an interrogator determined that a woman was Jewish based on the shape of her eyes, ears and, in particular, her nose. He had also indicated that one could identify our people by either their "full Jewish lips" or, conversely, their "thin Jewish lips."

All of the men from our Toloncház group underwent the examination. Predictably, the results were devastating – the examinations revealed that most of the men were Jewish. Only a handful, including Arthur, managed to fool the examiners. A combination of luck and quick thinking enabled a few of the men to position themselves and manipulate their organs in such a way that their circumcisions were not clear. A man could better explain this than I can. The result was that Arthur was among the few men who were not locked up that night. His brother Victor was not so fortunate.

The men who were locked up were to be deported the next day. But these men had already faced many hardships in their young lives and were not about to give up without a struggle. They hadn't gotten this far by being passive. That night, Victor and a few of the others tried to escape, taking quite a chance because they didn't know the area. They were caught and beaten mercilessly.

The following day, Victor was locked in a cattle car with other young men who, like him, were determined not to end up in Auschwitz. He told us later that one young man had managed to smuggle in a chain, which he concealed under his shirt. A group of men worked together tirelessly, using the chain to break open the car door. Finally, after two hours, they succeed in prying open the heavy door of the moving train. Some Jews who shared the car with them didn't jump out. They begged the young men to stay, fearing repercussions when the escape was discovered.

Not heeding these pleas, the men began to jump, one by one, from the speeding train. They jumped into the dark, moonless night, not knowing what lay below. They were travelling through eastern Slovakia, a rich lowland of barley, rye and wheat fields, and it was upon this hard earth that Victor landed. He felt a sharp pain in his elbow and knew at once he had broken something. Not knowing exactly where he was, he hid in some bushes until morning. As it turned out, he had jumped from the train very near my hometown, with which he was familiar. Some time later, with many escapades behind him, Victor joined the Slovak National Uprising. We learned of all of these things when we were reunited with him after the war.

From the time of the men's physical examinations, fate led me and Arthur down a different path from Victor's. That same evening of the examinations, we were again told to remain in our rooms until further notice. The next morning we were assembled in the courtyard and instructed to line up. The courtyard was a large area surrounded by buildings. In front of one building was a desk and two chairs. Two officers, one of them the commandant of the labour camp, sat behind the desk. He called out the names of those of us who remained, about seventy people in all. Then the commandant began to call the names again, in alphabetical order, beginning with women. It quickly became clear that anyone without documents, man or woman, was considered to be a Jew. In due course my name was called: Smutek, Helena. The commandant demanded to see my documents. Bravely, I told him, "I had my documents, but they were stolen." I thought this was a credible lie, but apparently the commandant did not. He dismissed me and I was directed to stand with the other women who had no papers. It looked like this would be the end for me.

Soon it was the men's turn to go and stand before this man who served as judge and jury. When Arthur's name was called, I watched him sadly as he approached the desk, marching confidently in military steps. As he spoke, Arthur's voice was quiet, but firm and clear. I could see that he had the commandant's full attention.

"Your name?" inquired the commandant, even though Arthur had come forward in response to his name having been called.

"Jan Orlinsky," replied Arthur.

"Your documents?"

"I have them!" Arthur declared.

"Yes, so show me," countered the commandant.

Arthur surprised everyone with his response. "You will get my documents tomorrow. I had KEOKH wire all of my documents to your attention."

KEOKH (the National Central Alien Control Office) was the office of the Ministry of Foreign Affairs that serviced legal aliens in Hungary – foreigners who had permits to remain in the country for a limited time. The commandant had probably never encountered such a situation in this little God-forsaken town. To receive a wire from the Ministry of Foreign Affairs in Budapest was a major event. The commandant seemed to accept that this was a possibility, but his next question showed that he still had doubts. "You have passed your physical examination, correct?"

"Correct," answered Arthur.

This was all the commandant needed to know. "You are free to go to the left," he said, glancing in the direction of those who had their documents. But Arthur did not move. "But sir, my fiancée is on the other side."

The commandant inquired, "Who is your fiancée? Show her to me."

"Helena Smutek," said Arthur, looking in my direction.

"Smutek, Helena!" barked the commandant. "Come stand beside Mr. Orlinsky!"

Arthur had saved my life yet again.

Once we were assigned to the "left" line, there was, amazingly, no follow-up. It didn't matter that Arthur's documents were non-existent; a few days later, accompanied by the police, we were again on our way to Budapest with twenty or so others. The Jews who had been assigned to the other line were eventually deported to Auschwitz. We had survived purgatory and emerged as bona fide Polish gentiles, who, as a result of the long-standing Hungarian-Polish friendship I mentioned, were often protected by Hungary.

Our next destination was Buda-Zugliget, a sizable military camp
for members of the decimated Polish army as well as anti-fascist Polish civilians. As a result of a de facto agreement between Hungary
and Poland, the camp had been established prior to the Nazi occupation to house Polish refugees so that they wouldn't fall into German
hands. It was the end of the summer of 1944 and we knew we weren't
out of the woods yet, that there were still dangers to face before we
reached the end of the war. I later learned that in less than three
months, between May and July 1944, approximately 450,000 Jews
had been deported from Hungary to Poland. Except for the majority
of the Jews of Budapest, who were concentrated in separate "yellow
star" housing and had been mostly untouched by the deportations,
Jews had been taken from throughout the country. But on October 15,
1944, in collaboration with Germany, the fascist Arrow Cross Party
took over the Hungarian government and after the coup, the next
phase began: the rounding up of the close to 250,000 Jews living in
Budapest.

Under the new fascist regime led by Ferenc Szálasi, there were
no more deportations from Budapest. Instead, Jews were rounded
up and ordered to do brutal forced labour, such as digging trenches,
without being given any food or water. The Nyilas now had simple,
inexpensive methods of killing and they were enthusiastic murderers
– they captured hundreds of Jews in roundups and herded them to
the shores of the Danube, where they shot them and threw them into
the river. At dawn, bodies often washed up on the shore.

In November 1944, the Americans and the Soviets began choking
the Nazis militarily, from both the west and the east. We could feel
that the war was coming to an end, but nobody knew exactly when.
The challenge was to not be caught in the final days of our ordeal.

I was still in Buda-Zugliget at this time, working as a typist and
interpreter at the Polish-Hungarian military headquarters. When we
had arrived there, along with primarily Polish civilians, the camp had
become responsible for us: we were registered and all of our records

were kept there. I, a.k.a. Helena Smutek, now had an official ID from the camp. And even better, Arthur and I were free to find our own lodgings in Budapest. Arthur found work in Nagykovácsi, a department store, and since I was believed to be completely bilingual, I was hired to work at the camp twice a week as a typist and occasionally as an interpreter. I tried to avoid doing the latter as much as possible because my skills in Polish were not up to those of a true Pole. Still, this job gave me the opportunity to keep on top of events, mainly by gaining information from other civilians.

My first month at Buda-Zugliget had been uneventful. Some time after that, some of us began to notice the disturbing presence of uniformed Nyilas in the camp. Within a few days we heard that a *razzia* would take place. This news was a shock to us. Why would they have a *razzia* in a place where there were supposedly no Jews? Those of us civilians who worked at the camp had to report to the administration every two weeks, so that they would know if we had fled. The *razzia* came on a day when we had come to pick up our bi-weekly pay, so the camp was full that day.

A Hungarian colonel who was also a physician approached me and directed me to join a group whom they believed to be Jewish. I had seen the colonel once or twice before at the camp offices. For some reason he decided that I was Jewish – he said it was the shape of my eyes that convinced him. My ID and explanations were of no help. I was taken to the same state security headquarters at Buda-Svábhegy where Arthur and I had gone when our apartment in Budapest had been raided just seven months earlier.

For the second time, I found myself in the place I most dreaded, about to be interrogated once again. I told myself to be smart. First, I would not acknowledge that I spoke Hungarian – when you speak more, you unwittingly reveal more. I also decided not to admit to having been there before. After all, who would remember me? Thousands of people came through there and I was sure there weren't any records other than the recollections in my head. I wouldn't confess to being Jewish this time, knowing it would mean certain death. How could I die now, after all we had managed to get through? I was determined that I would not allow myself to die by their bloody hands. These were the thoughts that pumped courage into my veins.

While waiting to be interrogated the next day, I was able to listen to the other women talking about their experiences. It was clear that those who firmly stuck to their stories, denying that they were Jewish, had lasted there much longer. We were kept in a mansion previously owned by a wealthy manufacturer. The family had been Hungarian nationalists, but they were anti-fascists. They had left Hungary just in time. If not for our horrible predicament, those of us incarcerated there would have enjoyed our surroundings, even in their deteriorated state.

The next day, a man came for me. As I walked out of the door, I went to turn in the direction I had seen the other Jewish women go, but I was stopped and instructed to go the other way. "Where am I going?" I wondered to myself. At the other end of the hall I was directed into an office where a typist sat behind one of two desks. She began by asking me about my knowledge of Hungarian. I told her I knew almost none, wondering all the while about this line of questioning. Had the colonel from the Polish military camp not reported his suspicions about my being Jewish? Did the right hand not know what the left hand was doing?

"We will need an interpreter," she said to the detective as he entered the room. But he felt that his Polish would be sufficient and that a translator wasn't necessary. The detective began by asking me to tell my story, starting with my childhood. He wanted to hear all of the details of my schooling, my early teen years, and on and on. I tried to use my best Polish. Suddenly, I was astonished to hear him ask me a question in Slovak. Of all people, I had been assigned to a Slovak detective! If he had been very attentive, he might have noticed many Slovak words interspersed with my Polish. But apparently he heard what he expected to hear from the young Polish woman who sat before him. Ironically, he looked pleased with his knowledge of Polish, remarking that he understood virtually everything I said! That's when I really began to sweat. I was questioned by him for two hours that day and two hours again the next. His questions were always variations of the same, as were my answers. I think he expected me to make a mistake when he sometimes repeated details from my life story, but he made no progress.

The third day, his questions were suddenly different. He inquired about my friends, my savings, my wardrobe. Did I socialize? With whom, how and when? All of a sudden he seemed to notice that my tinted blond hair had dark roots. He began to ask very insinuating questions about my life, to the point of being rude. Had we been speaking under different circumstances, I would have taken offence. Under the circumstances, however, some of his very transparent questions reassured me. I realized he was not talking to me as if he thought I was a Jew. He thought I was a spy!

The interrogation continued for a short while longer, until finally the detective informed me that he was obliged to search my living quarters before he could finalize my case. At first this seemed like good news to me. My room was small, dark and Spartan, not the accommodation of a high-living spy. But if we were to meet my landlords, that would be a problem, for I spoke fluent Hungarian with them. I rented a small room in their apartment and was on good terms with them. I often found myself turning when the man called his wife's name, which was also Zuzana. When people called out my wartime name, Helena, I sometimes needed to hear it twice before it registered. Since the detective thought I spoke little Hungarian, there would be grave consequences if I were to encounter them that day.

As we entered my building, I began to shake and perspire. Would this be the end for me? I couldn't picture it all concluding this way, otherwise I might have tried to escape onto the streets. On the eleventh floor, I opened the door to my apartment, number fifteen. Looking around, I realized at once that no one was home. Another miracle! Once again, there was a good force behind me. I was discharged for lack of evidence.

～

Not long after my short stint as a suspected spy, Arthur and I began looking for new lodgings. We had no references to provide, but after interviewing us a few times, a woman named Mrs. Merish decided to rent us a room in her spacious apartment. For this discriminating lady, we had the best possible reference – the Nagykovácsi department store, where Arthur worked, was well known for its unconditional support of the fascist regime. It gave considerable financial donations to the Arrow Cross Party and it had a long-standing policy of not hiring Jews. During the war, the store managers intensified their employee screening process, but they also had a shortage of workers for manual labour so they had turned to the Polish-Hungarian military camps for a supply of strong, young men, which is how Arthur got his job. Mrs. Merish wouldn't have been so impressed had she known that Arthur's job consisted of hauling garbage, chopping wood and moving heavy boxes and furniture.

Nagykovácsi was the perfect hiding place. No one looked for "undesirable" people there. Wanting to limit our exposure to the outside world, we had deliberately searched for a place to live within a four-block radius of the store. It was difficult to find a room for rent because so many buildings had been inundated with people seeking shelter. We went from building to building and street to street, seeking out building superintendents who could tell us which tenants might be willing to rent out a room. When we found Mrs. Merish, we thought she would be a safe landlady. At seventy, we didn't expect her to be actively interested in politics. It turned out we were wrong.

Mrs. Merish had a special place on her wall reserved for a picture of her son, who was fighting alongside the German army on the Eastern Front. She told us that her son was fighting for a just cause, saying that it would be better to die than to live under Jewish communist rule. She had raised him with these attitudes and now supported his role in the war with great élan. He was not just her only child, he was her only living relative. And, as if her championing the fascist cause wasn't enough to turn our stomachs, we also discovered that she kept a revolver in her night table, "just in case."

Her ardent support of fascist ideology included worshipping the Szálasi government and Hitler, whose pictures were hanging on the walls of her living room, along with one of her son. Each was adorned with red, white and green ribbons, the national colours of Hungary.

It seemed to me that her nationalism was actually a form of escapism. In her earlier years, Mrs. Merish had been somebody – the third wife and widow of a much-loved Hungarian music icon. In the past she had enjoyed wealth and status, with a social circle that included aristocrats of influence. But Mrs. Merish was now isolated from this high society as the result of being widowed, making bad financial investments and holding strong political views. By the time we met her, Mrs. Merish didn't have any friends. She also didn't mix with others in the building. She felt that none of her neighbours were good enough for her.

Ironically, Mrs. Merish was fascinated by our fictitious backgrounds. I think it pleased her to believe we were who she wanted us to be. Before the war, we told her, Arthur had been a forester, overseeing the woods belonging to Graf Potocki, a well-known Polish aristocrat. This greatly impressed Mrs. Merish. As for me, our story was that my Hungarian mother had married a Pole, which explained why I was fluent in Hungarian. Mrs. Merish thought Arthur's broken Hungarian was cute and, as a couple, she viewed us as the perfect example of Polish-Hungarian friendship.

We could feel that the end of the war was slowly coming close. Nonetheless, as the war entered its final stages, taking its last weakened breaths, the Hungarian fascists were still shooting Jews and throwing the corpses into the Danube. We weren't safe yet. We avoided Mrs. Merish as much as possible. Every Sunday we went out for several hours, wanting to give her the impression we were regular church-goers. She never asked us questions, but watched us intently. As Christmas approached, we began to worry. Our lack of knowledge of the holiday rituals would give us away. We knew that it was customary for families to celebrate the occasion by spending Christmas Eve together. To sit with her then would surely have been suicidal.

We needed to find a way to keep our distance over the course of the holiday. Being a woman, I knew what would likely make her angry enough to avoid us. The agreement we had in sharing her kitchen was that we clean up after ourselves. The day before Christmas I used the kitchen, deliberately leaving the stove dirty and dishes in the sink. I knew she would be furious, which she was, so much so that she didn't speak to me. The plan worked! I also made a point of letting her see me with our small plastic Christmas tree in my hands.

At dinner that night in our room, as we ate our cauliflower soup – a meagre treat for the occasion – I remembered a carol that my family's domestic help had sung in my childhood. Recalling two of the verses, I sang the melody over and over, for what felt like an hour, knowing Mrs. Merish could hear me in the next room. Then Arthur sang a melody unfamiliar to me, reading sentences backward from a German newspaper, hoping that our landlady would think it was a Polish Christmas carol!

The next morning, believing that the characters we had assumed would go to morning mass, we prepared to go to St. Stephen's Basilica. We met Mrs. Merish in the kitchen, wished her a Merry Christmas and gave her a small jar of plum compote. She, in turn, presented us with a jar of marmalade and mentioned how much she enjoyed listening to my Christmas carol. Oddly enough, in spite of her deep religious feelings, she didn't go out to mass that morning, although she didn't discourage us from going. We left feeling puzzled but sure that in our position, it was the right thing to do.

Only later, out on the deserted streets of Budapest, did we realize how contemptible it was of her to let us go out, as we were clearly unaware that there was a curfew in effect. Mrs. Merish owned a radio and she knew that we did not. As we walked, we heard an amplified voice warning people to stay home in light of the treacherous situation on the streets. The voice told us that the city was temporarily surrounded by the Soviet enemy, but that it wouldn't be long before our superior army pushed them back.

But there was no turning back now. We were already far down the street, although still a few kilometres from the Basilica. As shells fell on the city, covering the sidewalks and streets with shattered glass, we continued, knowing that we might easily be hit. We had no choice but to continue, for there was nowhere to stop. No shops were open, the lavatories located under the streets were closed, and we didn't know anyone who lived along the way. After the war, we learned that on that Christmas morning, the city was surrounded on three sides, with only the west side open, allowing the German army to retreat in that direction.

As we walked, the shelling was unquestionably frightening, but the danger we feared most was the armed Nyilas patrols. If we encountered them while scurrying on suspiciously under such circumstances, we knew we could end up in the Danube. This journey wasn't the smartest thing we did during our time in Budapest. As we walked, we didn't encounter any other civilians, only guards standing outside the gates of important buildings. Eventually, we were spotted by a patrol, who asked us where we were heading. The officer was taken aback by our reply, but didn't stop us from continuing on our way.

When we finally arrived at our destination, Arthur and I were exhausted. The Basilica was a major tourist attraction, built in the style of St. Peter's in Rome. It could accommodate thousands of worshippers but on that morning, there were only ten people assembled, including the priest and ourselves. There was no mass scheduled at all.

On the journey back to our room, Arthur and I tried to take shortcuts, but twice still managed to come across Nyilas patrols who eyed us suspiciously. When we returned to our room, drained and despondent, we slept until the evening. That night, the building superintendent decided that we all had to move our most necessary belongings to the bomb shelter and remain there for a time.

It didn't escape Arthur's and my attention that Mrs. Merish chose a place at the opposite end from us in the shelter. From then on she didn't approach us or even look at us. Could she have had a guilty conscience? We didn't understand how she could have allowed us to go out like that. A humane person wouldn't have even sent out their dog under such conditions. This incident revealed her true character and her lack of concern for others around her. After analyzing the situation, I decided that she was now avoiding us because her deep religious beliefs had caused her to feel ashamed. Her silence that Christmas morning could have cost us our lives.

Liberation and Loss

Many people, when they look back on the end of the war, remember it as a time when people were dancing and kissing in the streets. But that kind of response was the reaction of those who were far removed from the cruel realities of the war. Most Europeans and North Americans were tired of the whole thing and looked forward to getting on with their lives. Eastern European Jews like us were more cautious – relieved to be alive, of course, but where were all the others? We wondered who among our dispersed families and friends had survived. I especially wanted to know about my father. Where was he? I didn't feel joyous or that I deserved happiness. It was hard to believe that at the end of the war I was only twenty years old. I felt three times older.

For us, the war didn't reach a dramatic conclusion. It felt as though the fighting in Budapest simply stopped. The morning of January 18, 1945, we left the shelter to find the streets eerily silent. Our shelter had withstood the bombings, but the rest of the building stood with naked walls exposed to the open sky. We had been liberated! We had survived!

Cautiously, we approached the iron gates at the front of the building. I can still remember how the pavement was covered with snow when we saw a Soviet soldier walking slowly across the street. Was this a dream? We looked at him in awe. He represented everything we wanted from life: to live like human beings, to be free. We had to touch him, to see if he was real. "Will you be staying here? Will there be a retreat?" Arthur asked him in Rusyn, an East Slavic language that the soldier could understand. He reassured us that the Germans were gone for good.

On the second day of our freedom, we ventured out further, although we were warned that it was still dangerous. There was a lot to worry about – mines, bombs, fascists, communists, thieves, disease from dead people and animals in the streets, and so on. Despite the warnings, we went out. We had waited for this day for so long, through all the years of the war, missing our youth, torn from loved ones and the lives we had known. Our bodies had survived intact, but our eyes remained wet with tears for most of that day.

The narrow downtown street along which we walked had tall buildings on both sides, all damaged by the battle. It was a sunny winter's day. In the distance we still heard shooting, but here there was only silence. Further along we came across a large military truck, surrounded by Soviet soldiers. From a distance, we watched as they loaded the truck with leather goods from a store. Suddenly, the group's leader noticed us and beckoned for us to come closer. "Are you two the owners of this store?" he asked. "No, Captain, we are not," answered Arthur. "We have never seen this store before." "So why are you watching us?" he demanded. "Get on the truck! We will take you to the commandant to find out more about you." "Captain," said Arthur, "we are not watching what you are doing, we are watching out of happiness that you have liberated us."

The captain wasn't impressed. He became impatient and wanted us to get onto the truck. Arthur tried again. "Captain, we are not Hungarian, we are Czechoslovakian! Friends!" He said this knowing that the Soviets felt no warmth toward Hungarians. "If that is so," replied the captain, "what are you doing here? Why aren't you fighting the Germans?" "We are Jews," we answered. "We survived the war here. We are very happy to see you!" It took some time before he relented to our pleas to be let go. Then he said, "Go home, and don't come out on the streets for a while."

Later we learned that many Jews in similar situations, believing that the Soviets wouldn't harm them, were taken to Siberia. Some never returned, and others made their way home only five or ten years later. This might have served as a warning about our future under a communist regime.

In the days following Budapest's liberation, we concentrated our thoughts on finally returning home, although for a time we continued to live in the bomb shelter of Mrs. Merish's building. Throughout the war, and in the months after, an apartment building's superintendent was in a position of power. His presence was more important than the landlord's, whom the tenants rarely saw. During the war, a superintendent was someone to be respected and feared. He could save or destroy lives, depending on his nature and political biases. Superintendents were frequently offered bribes by local police or other officials and tenants. The responsibility for distributing food-rationing stamps was also under the superintendent's jurisdiction, which meant that he had control not only over the roof above the tenants' heads but also over the food they ate.

We considered our superintendent to be the best, one of the good ones. Somehow we knew that he passively resisted the fascist regime. When we had first moved in to Mrs. Merish's we'd seen compassion for us in his eyes, as if he was silently conveying to us that he knew we were not who we pretended to be and that he was our friend. Our luck in having him in charge of our building cannot be overstated. After the war, we discovered that he was part of the Social Democratic Party, which had been declared illegal once the Nazis invaded. There was really very little underground activity on the part of leftist groups in Hungary during the war, but his political sentiments clearly affected his daily interactions.

On many evenings, small groups of soldiers wandered into our building. Our superintendent usually looked after them, keeping them happy by providing hospitality as best he could. The Soviet soldiers who occupied Budapest behaved in the same way as other victorious military forces have been known to – looting, drinking and womanizing – not necessarily in any particular order. One night our superintendent was worried about a violent group of soldiers who would be drinking and staying in his apartment on the main floor. He cautioned the tenants and suggested that women who had somewhere else to go for the night should leave quickly, since he couldn't guarantee that he would be able to keep the group under reasonable control.

We had recently become friends with an older, quite religious Hungarian gentile couple who had lost their only son in one of Budapest's early air raids. After he passed away, the couples' life seemed to lose all meaning and the only thing that prevented them from giving up on life was their deep piety. Our friend Mary was in her early seventies. Although she was only skin and bones and looked older than her years, she was concerned for our safety and suggested that she and I go to her friend Anna's building nearby. So far, no soldiers had made themselves at home on her street.

I remember that it was very cold the night that Mary and I moved into the shelter of Anna's building. The only warmth we had was from what we wore – winter coats and shawls wrapped around our heads and necks. In the shelter there were only three candles providing dim light. Anna offered us her bed, which was next to her husband's, and she moved into his.

It was around midnight when we heard loud knocking at the entrance to the shelter. Two drunken soldiers barged in, making the noise of ten men. Oh God, I thought, what will happen to us now? It was believed that soldiers did not accost women in bed with their husbands. Mary and I were perfect choices for the soldiers, however, as we were two women in bed without a man.

The soldiers used flashlights to view the occupants of the beds. After surveying the shelter one of them returned to our bed. I looked at him and began to speak in broken Russian.

"I am sick." I told him in a low voice.

"Yes?" he replied, waiting for me to go on.

"I have typhoid fever." I continued, sticking out my tongue and forcing strange noises to come from my throat. My declaration did not appear to have deterred him. I tried my next weapon. "Comrade," I said. "I am Czechoslovakian!" "Good!" he answered. "Then we are kin!"

Then, as suddenly as they had arrived, they were gone. I couldn't understand what had happened. What had been their intentions? The others in the shelter, not understanding Russian, thought I had said something to make them leave. They were excited and wanted to know who I was. I had unwittingly become an asset. For my part, I just hoped that the men would not come back. But an hour later, they did.

In the middle of the shelter stood two chairs and a small table. The soldiers sat down and put two bottles of hard liquor on the table. Clearly they had gone out to get more to drink. At that moment, I noticed that Anna's husband was alone in their bed. "Where is Anna?" I whispered. "She is with me, hidden under the comforter. We don't trust them," he said. I knew this was my chance, if I acted fast. Without another word, I jumped into his bed, knowing I would be safer in bed with a man. Anna lay quietly at his feet, but her husband was furious.

"What are you doing?" he demanded.

"Please be quiet!" I answered. "You don't have to worry. Your wife is safe." I pulled the shawl tighter to cover my face.

The soldiers emptied their bottles and proclaimed, "Aludni!" In Hungarian this means it is time to sleep. One of the now very intoxicated soldiers approached the bed where Mary now lay alone. Suddenly she realized the position she was in: one woman alone in a bed. I had acted quickly on impulse to save myself, but now I worried about Mary. The soldier came closer and pulled the blanket off of her. She was fully dressed, in her clothes and coat, as was the soldier.

Without bothering to remove his weapon, the soldier fell on top of Mary and, thank God, within a second fell asleep, snoring loudly.

Anna, Mary and I felt this was the time to get out of there. We left the shelter and ran up the stairs to sit on the living room sofa in what was once Anna's apartment. The roof was gone and the stars were shining above our heads and the night air was frigid. Although she hadn't been assaulted, Mary felt deeply humiliated. She begged us not to tell her husband of the incident. We would tell him that we had spent a quiet night sleeping in Anna's shelter, with no disruptions from unruly soldiers. Mary and I returned home again at dawn.

Arthur and I remained with Mary and her husband at the shelter in Mrs. Merish's building for another two weeks or so. They never knew we were Jewish. When we left them it was still as Jan Orlinsky and Helena Smutek, the Polish couple. Ten years after the war, we visited Mary. Her husband was no longer alive. It wasn't necessary to reveal our true identities to a woman of her age; we parted again, as Jan and Helena.

~

That spring, when the war was truly over, we decided that there was no longer any reason for us to prolong our stay in Budapest. It was a pity, since Budapest was always at its most beautiful in spring, when the flowers were in full bloom. I remember the scent was so breathtaking that at times it camouflaged the noxious smell of car exhaust. In 1945, the month of May was even nicer than usual; it was as if Mother Nature wanted to contribute to the celebrations that marked the official end of the war. The wide avenues of Budapest were overflowing with people marching and chanting the *Internationale*, the anthem sung by communist workers around the world. People joyously celebrated the victory of the Allies. In the midst of the euphoria, we also mourned the passing of US President Franklin D. Roosevelt, whom we had naively considered the saviour of the Jews.

Arthur and I ached to get home quickly to find any family members who had survived. We packed our meagre belongings and departed from Arthur's cousin's home, where we had been staying for about two months after leaving Mary and her husband. It was the middle of May when we boarded an overcrowded, dirty train at Eastern Railway Station, waiting for three hours since the departure time was delayed. I was looking out the window, breathing in the heavily polluted air filled with train and tobacco smoke, when suddenly I heard a desperate-sounding voice calling out our names. It was Victor! He had made the journey to Budapest to find Arthur, and their cousin had hastily directed him to the station – if the train had run on time, Victor would have missed us.

As one would imagine, our reunion with Victor was highly emotional. When we recovered our composure, we were eager to hear each other's experiences during the time we had been separated. Victor knew the fate of almost everyone in our families. The most important thing to me was that he knew what had happened to my father, whom Victor had briefly met back in Humenné when my father was on one of his leaves from the labour camp. Victor had spent two weeks or so with my father in the mountains of central Slovakia in September 1944. It was near the beginning of the Slovak National Uprising and most of the remaining younger Jews from labour camps, or those who had been in hiding, were eager to be a part of the resistance. Victor was soon engaged in real fighting and my father fled deep into the mountains with a large group of people his age.

In just over two months, the ill-prepared and short-lived uprising was crushed. It was then that my father was caught by the Germans and taken with many others to a nearby town. Victor didn't know how he had perished. Some people were shot and thrown into a mass grave; others were taken to an active, burning lime pit and thrown alive into the flames. Although we never found out how my dear father died, I have always hoped that he didn't end his days in this horrible way.

Arthur and Victor's middle brother, Eman, had also been in a labour camp but had managed to obtain an exemption allowing him to use his professional skills to help build hotels in the High Tatra Mountains. He joined the Slovak National Uprising as well, where he temporarily reunited with Victor, but was captured and deported to Germany, where he was sent to a forced labour camp. He survived and found us once he made his way back to Slovakia after the war. Out of all the other members of Arthur and Victor's family, only Eman had survived. Their parents and four sisters had perished in the camps.

The initial euphoria of our reunion with Victor passed. All three of us were miserable as we faced the news of what had become of so many of our loved ones. Perhaps we were numb, but I remember feeling that there was no longer any reason to rush home. The three of us spent another month in Budapest before we decided to return to Humenné.

~

When Arthur, Victor and I finally made our way to Humenné, I visited my old gentile neighbours who had saved a few of my family's belongings, things of sentimental value. The photographs, in particular, were priceless to me. The enormity of my loss had not yet sunk in. I got great pleasure from browsing through the pictures of my family, especially those of my mother in her younger, healthy days, taking a cure for some gynecological difficulties at a well-known spa. Seeing these pictures reminded me why I had been so cherished by my parents. Although I was an only child, my mother had delivered other children before my birth: a baby girl who lived only two weeks and a premature boy who was stillborn. Subsequently, she had had two miscarriages. It was easy to understand why they had doted on me.

I still have and treasure many of these photographs that were saved for me. When I look at them I recall my mother talking with pleasure about the happy times in Budapest with my parents' siblings and their families. I enjoy seeing pictures of my cousins and me. When I looked at these pictures after the war, I saw beyond the smiling faces and remembered the lives they had lived. I envisioned the past, before the war, before the Nazis, and relived those moments again and again. Those days, along with many of the people I loved, are gone forever.

Sadly, among all the pictures I discovered only one of my father, taken for his passport. Actually, it shouldn't have been a surprise that there were almost no photographs of him. Papa was a devout, practicing Jew and traditional Judaism teaches that one should not make replicas of humans, since this is God's privilege alone. For many pious Jews, images in human form can be considered idolatrous. In practical terms this meant no photographs or watching movies, which today would include television. And so I am left with just the one photo of my father, Samuel Weinberger.

It is clear that my father didn't impose this tradition on the rest of the family because, in addition to family photographs, I found many of my school pictures taken at the end of each year. Studying the photographs closely, I counted that up until Grade 8, there were twenty-four Jewish students out of a total of thirty-eight in my class. The rest were Czechs and poor Slovak children whose families could not afford the private Catholic school. In 1939, the ratio changed. The Czechs were gone, forced to leave Slovakia, and, out of thirty-two students, only eight Jews remained.

As I browsed through the photographs of my friends, girls and boys aged fifteen to eighteen, I reflected on what had become of them. Many had perished soon after the first transports arrived in Auschwitz. I could still see some of them so vividly. How could they have died so young? What beasts the Nazis were! Look what they did to us.

There was a picture of Ida. I wonder if we realized then what a pretty girl she was. Maybe we didn't acknowledge it because we were jealous. She was always surrounded by an entourage of the three best-looking boys in town. They would wait for her, all three of them, in front of her house, and then walk with her up and down the main street promenade, with Ida in her impeccable clothing. She came from a wealthy family and liked to show off her wardrobe. I remember how marvellous she looked in her smart, green coat with the Persian black collar. Ida was very attractive, with red hair, a fair complexion and shapely legs. We used to tease her about her freckles but, in truth, on her they looked pretty. Ida was one of the few women that went into hiding instead of going with the first women's transport. She was caught later and didn't survive.

There was also a picture of me with my schoolmate Annie, wearing our yellow bands on our coat sleeves in 1940. Annie was the one that was with me the day we went to Eva's house and had that inane conversation with Eva's father. Annie wasn't the best of students, but she was a good sport. She was an only child, like me. Her family had come to Humenné from another town. It's funny, the things that stand out in one's memory. Annie's parents were very friendly and I recall one occasion in particular when I was invited to their home for lunch. Much to my surprise, Annie's mother served pork goulash. There was no way I could eat the meal. I had never eaten pork, I told her, begging not to be forced to start now.

Annie's mother patiently explained to me that it was all in my head, that I would find that I had never eaten such a delicious goulash and I would ask for a second helping. She was so persistent that I finally gave in. With the full bowl of goulash before me, I ate a spoonful, then a second and a third. Annie's mother sat opposite me, watching every bite. Spoon number four, number five.... then my stomach lurched and I knew that I needed to get away from the table quickly. I ran from the room and threw up in their backyard. I was sick the whole afternoon and my parents were very upset about the incident. My friend Annie was another one who didn't survive.

Among the precious photographs was also a picture of Vera, our landlord's daughter. At the time it was taken, she was about twelve. She was smart and well-behaved, and her family made it their business to convince the whole town that they were very serious about converting to Christianity. The family went to church each day and even their children believed that their conversion was real. They took lessons and did all that was required for their conversion. Even though the Jewish Code clearly indicated that they were still Jewish, everyone did what they could to survive. It was known to everyone, even the highest officials, how dedicated Vera's family was to their adopted religion. Their conversion seemed to have paid off, for the family hadn't been forced from their home. If we had all known that Humenné would have a selective interpretation of the Jewish Code, perhaps more of us would have made better use of these conversions.

One day, Vera came into our kitchen while I was frying some minced meat. She was a good eater and took one of the cooked burgers from the plate. Suddenly her face turned red, she stopped chewing and spit out her mouthful of meat. I asked her what was wrong and she replied, "It's Friday. I have committed a terrible sin to have eaten meat on a Friday!" I don't know much about what happened to Vera later in the war, but when Humenné was evacuated as the Soviet front moved closer, Vera's family fled to the central part of Slovakia. She now lives a happy life in Israel.

There were also pictures of Marta and Irina, my oldest friends. Marta's family minded their own business and raised obedient children. When the Nazis invaded, their family decided that they would either live or die together. With two young children under ten, Marta sick with tuberculosis and a mother with heart problems, they stood little chance of surviving. The oldest son, a medical student, had been their hope for the future. The whole family was murdered in Auschwitz.

Irina and I had always been competitive. We compared who had the highest marks, the most friends, who sat beside the teacher in the class photo, and on and on. Irina's family responded to the crisis differently. To save her from the single women's transport, they had found her a husband. Their intention was that it would be a marriage on paper only. After her marriage we met once on the street and I recognized that familiar look of triumph in her eyes – she had been first to marry, at the young age of seventeen. The marriage not only saved Irina from being deported with the single women, but it also ended up becoming real – the two fell in love and lived together happily. At eighteen, Irina had a baby. Sadly, the little family didn't have long to be together. They too met their death in the Auschwitz gas chambers.

I also have a photograph of Laco. He was a pleasant young man with a slight frame. He was an ardent member of Betar, a right-wing Zionist organization, and he promoted its militant ideology verbally and financially. Many times Laco tried, in vain, to get out of Slovakia. He had a stepbrother in the United Kingdom, but the bureaucracy was so slow that he could never catch a train to his freedom. He spent two years in Auschwitz and other camps, miraculously surviving the war in spite of his fragile build. Tragically, after liberation, Laco lost his final battle to typhus, which he contracted just one week after he had been freed.

Another face among the photos was Viola. She was naive and had reported for the first single women's transport, believing with all her heart that they would be taken to work in the shoe factory in Baťovany near Humenné. She knew that they wouldn't be paid for their work but felt they would be safe and even have fun, all those girls together. Viola wasn't alone in her beliefs. So many wanted to believe that no harm would come to them. Even Viola's parents clung to this view of events. When all of the young women began to enter the cattle car Viola panicked, realizing she had left her new expensive leather boots behind. She ran home for them and, still believing she was headed for the shoe factory, returned in time for the transport's departure. She was apparently among the first to be gassed at Auschwitz.

And then there was the picture of Hannah. Even seeing the picture today, some fifty years later, I recall a moment of childhood pain. Perhaps this incident stands out in my mind because it was so ordinary compared to what was to come in the future. On December 6, our school celebrated St. Nicholas Day. For the occasion the school rented a large hall where we were to enjoy plays and various performances. At the end, presents were exchanged – friend to friend, teacher to teacher, student to teacher. Hannah told me to bring her a gift and she, in turn, would get one for me. I planned to buy her chocolate, nicely wrapped in coloured cellophane, but I needed a crown, which was a great deal of money in those days. My father wasn't pleased. Why did I need a whole crown? He reminded me how hard a person must work to earn a crown and said that I was going to spend it on nothing. I was young, though, and persistent. In the end, I got my crown.

The big moment arrived and the teacher in charge called us by name to come to the stage and receive our presents. I was given a large box, which was very light. I took it home to open it. Inside the big box was a smaller box, and inside this box was another still smaller one. Finally I found a lid from a tin of shoe cream. I was so hurt and ashamed. My poor hard-working father had given me a crown for nothing. To this day I remember how deeply disappointed I was. Hannah avoided me after that and we never interacted after that day.

I heard that Hannah spent three years in concentration camps. She was among the few women I knew who survived. After the war she moved to Prague where she lived with her husband and two daughters.

Looking through these pictures in Humenné after the war, I knew this would never again be home for me. I had the photos to remind me of the life we once had there, a life that was now lost and broken. I was ready to face the reality that I had to move on.

Rebuilding Our Life

After our brief stop in Humenné where we faced the reality of who had made it home and who would never return, we decided to move to Bratislava, a city in southwestern Slovakia about five hundred kilometers away. No one we knew there had been compromised by their activities during the war. Both Victor and Eman eventually joined us and we remained there for twenty-three years. Some survivors spent their entire lifetimes looking back. We continued to hear mind-boggling stories that ended in either tragedy or miracle. Only real life could produce tales of such magnitude – no writer could have created a more horrific story. As for Arthur and me, we were healed by looking ahead.

A few months after the official end of the war, the world began to judge the demons who had instigated the atrocities. Everyone was now aware of the scope of the Holocaust. For many, the war crimes trials that began in the fall of 1945 were a satisfying ending, a victory of good over evil. Young and old alike began to see the future more brightly. The world had had enough of grey clouds and shadows.

What a pity that so many close to our hearts – the parents, siblings, classmates and friends whom we had lost – could not witness the reparations for the devastating losses we had experienced. Many survivors were entitled to accommodations and medical care provided by social service agencies. And an assistance plan run by the

United Nations Relief and Rehabilitation Administration (UNRRA) had begun, providing food and shelter for the staggering number of refugees who no longer had homes to go back to.

People slowly began to resettle. Hardly anyone remained in their native towns. It would have been like witnessing the past at every turn. We used to say it was like a migration of the nations. Many people were on the move from different parts of the world and many found loved ones and made new acquaintances in new places. Only a significant upheaval can cause such masses of people to move. World War II was just such a cataclysm.

Arthur and I were married in Humenné on July 30, 1945. We had our honeymoon, a few days of well-deserved rest, in a resort in the High Tatra Mountains, Slovakia's Alps. One evening, in the recreation centre of the resort, we met a young woman who had arrived the day before. Her face bore a look of misery and there was nothing youthful in the way she carried her body. The young woman's name was Marta and she was at the resort attempting to recover. Her tragedy had taken place only recently, not quite two months after the end of the war. We hoped her story would be one of the last cries we heard from the war.

She had been part of a group of five young women, sisters and cousins, all survivors of the Nazi death march following the evacuation of Auschwitz, on their way home to the eastern part of Czechoslovakia after the end of the war. They had a long way to go and were using every means of transportation available, especially the railway. In spite of the re-established railway administration, the system was chaotic and inefficient. The women sometimes found themselves sitting in a train car in front of a train station for an entire day. Trains at that time were still largely engaged in the dismantling of the war.

The young women finally made it to their village and all happily rushed home. Upon their arrival, many friends and neighbours gathered in front of their house, laughing, crying and reminiscing. The women then entered their house and found most of the furniture had been broken. Fortunately, there were two beds side by side, which could accommodate them all. Other than some utensils in the kitchen, the rest of the house was in ruins.

They began to discuss their futures: what to do, where to go, how to contact relatives overseas. They were so young and without parents. Sitting on the beds, the young women listened carefully to each other's stories, some told over and over again. With eyes and ears wide open, they laughed and cried together. They were young and excited, fully expecting to make a complete recovery and a fresh start.

The next day, the young women spent the day talking about their childhoods, reminiscing about life with their parents and siblings. It had been a hard, rural existence, balanced each week by the Sabbath, a day of peace and religious observance. They affirmed that the love and closeness of their families had made a life that was difficult seem much easier.

Each night they slept in different combinations. Attempting to squeeze five into the two connected beds, they had discovered that it was most comfortable if the shortest one slept with her head at the bottom of the bed. It was Marta who slept with her head at the foot of the bed, so she was totally covered by a comforter, in spite of the warm night. One night, Marta awoke, hearing a noise. She froze, although she didn't know exactly what she had heard. Suddenly the doors were forced open and two drunken men with handguns entered the room.

They immediately saw the four young women in the bed. Not realizing that a fifth one was under the comforter, they threw their guns and the blanket on top of her and proceeded to rape the other four. When they were finished, they began to shoot in all directions, even at the ceiling. Then they departed as quickly as they had come.

A long time passed, with a deafening silence hanging in the air. Marta told us she didn't know how long she lay still, not daring to move. When she became aware of the lifeless bodies beside her, she jumped from the bed. She was covered in blood but didn't feel as though she had been wounded. The bullets had missed her. Marta then lost consciousness.

She awoke later in a hospital. Realizing what had happened, Marta wanted to run away. She wondered what beasts had done this. Would they be caught and punished? What had happened to the bodies of her relatives? These questions pounded in her head, but she was unable to utter them.

Marta's group was not the only one attacked that night in the village. Eighteen Jewish survivors lost their lives at the hands of a group of drunken men. They rounded up the men, raped the women and then shot them all. Marta realized that she had now survived a second time. It was miraculous that she had not been shot. Yet her soul was shot, with a wound that would be impossible to heal.

People said that this vicious, cowardly attack was perpetrated by a group called the *banderowcy*, or *bandera*, named after their leader. Apparently they were mostly army deserters and Ukrainian nationalists – misfits who regularly got drunk and carried out attacks in the middle of the night. For six months or so after the war the members of this group terrorized the southeast of Poland, the Ukraine and areas near the Carpathian Mountains, into eastern Czechoslovakia. The *banderas* only targeted Jews who had survived the camps.

～

After the war, settling in Bratislava and starting our family, Arthur and I began to build a new life on the remnants of our old, broken world. Our new life came with its daily challenges, such as finding a decent place to live, looking for jobs, and last but not least, raising our four children, Tamara, Paul, Michael and Matthew, who were born in 1946, 1948, 1950 and 1953, respectively. When the 1948 Communist coup occurred, we were not overly concerned – we had been liberated by the Soviets, we felt that the worst was behind us, and we were both working enough to meet our basic needs. I worked as a clerk in the civil engineering section of the Scientific Technical Society, and

Arthur, after first working as a journalist and then a librarian, became a researcher at an institution for water management.

In 1958, my office hired a new typist by the name of Jana. Although it was her first job, Jana had excellent skills and a pleasant disposition. She was also interesting, learned quickly and very soon felt at home in the office. Her porcelain complexion and curly brown hair made her lovely to look at in spite of the long scar which ran from the top of her forehead to the bridge of her nose. Jana had bangs – presumably to cover the scar – but it was visible most of the time because her unruly hair didn't stay in place. The scar looked like it had been there for a long time.

In time, I learned that Jana was married to a physician. They had a good relationship and were blessed with two young children. In spite of our age difference – Jana was twenty-five years old when she came to work in the office – we became close. We always had a great deal to talk about: politics, cooking, our children, our health and harmless gossip. Other than speaking of her children, Jana said little about her private life and never touched on the past. I respected that and never asked prying questions. Jana remained with the company for a little more than a year.

Almost thirty years later, in 1988, our four children arranged a Mediterranean cruise for Arthur and me. On the fourth day of the cruise, while strolling on the deck, much to my surprise, I bumped into Jana, my old friend and colleague. Although we hadn't seen each other for so long and the time showed on both of our faces, we nonetheless recognized each other immediately. It was a joyful reunion. As the saying goes, it's a small world.

Jana was alone on the cruise but I found out that she and her husband lived in Toronto, not far from us. Her children lived out of town. It turned out that Jana had recently been released from a psychiatric hospital. Although I was genuinely shocked, I tried not to show it. She seemed well, but apparently was still taking medication.

Later, under the refuge of darkness, Jana shared more of her story.

The sea was peaceful and a gentle breeze caressed our faces as she opened up to me. The events of her past were revealed little by little, as we met almost every night after that. It all came out easily, without any pressure on my part. I hoped that talking about her experiences would not cause her any further harm.

At great length Jana described her childhood in Slovakia, the years with her parents, brother and her paternal aunt. Her father and aunt had inherited the house where they all lived. Jana's aunt was an important member of the family and played a significant role in her and her brother's lives. The source of the family's livelihood was a store in a nearby city. Her parents left for the store early each morning and returned late in the evening, leaving the children in their aunt's care. Their lives were predictable and typical of the times.

By the time Jana was nine, in 1942, the Nazi regime had liquidated the store and her family's life changed drastically. Their schooling, work and movements were totally restricted. She didn't need to elaborate, for I had experienced this first-hand as well. When the deportations began, Jana's family discussed the situation but they were divided about a plan for their survival. The parents believed that there was nothing they could do but go with the transports. Jana's aunt decided to stay behind with the children, in hiding. Who knew which was the right choice? No one was able to predict what lay ahead.

The day that the Hlinka Guard began rounding up people for their designated transport, Jana's parents waited on the porch. They were taken to Auschwitz while the three remaining family members hid in a small room in the basement. Their aunt had prepared ahead by storing supplies such as flour, corn, oil, sugar and potatoes. There was a stove and two narrow sofas, sufficient for their needs. The biggest problem for them was lack of ventilation. At night they had to open the doors for some air. During the day, when the door to their hiding place was closed, the entrance was well hidden. They thought no one would suspect that there was an entrance in the wall behind the kitchen. Jana told me that they were careful, trying to use electricity as little as possible.

After a month in hiding, two Hlinka Guards broke down the main doors of their house. Jana's brother was upstairs and had left the door to their hiding place open. All three were caught. Jana recalled that it was the middle of September and the days were getting shorter. They were taken away late in the afternoon when it was already growing dark. She and her brother and aunt were put on a truck with twenty other people, some of whom she recognized. Not far from town, they were unloaded from the truck in front of a small forest where more people were gathered.

The crowd was pushed into the woods, behind the tall pine trees. Jana knew this place, having often gone there for day trips in the summer. But it looked different now. Ahead of them was a clearing and in the middle of it was a freshly dug deep and narrow pit. They were ordered to face the pit. As Jana was only nine, she didn't know what was about to happen. Her aunt did and pulled Jana's thin body in front of her own ample frame so she couldn't be seen from behind. Jana told me that she held her brother's hand as he stood to her left. The sun had almost finished setting when the shooting began.

She must have been unconscious for some time; she doesn't know how long she lay beneath her aunt's dead body. It was hard for Jana to tell this part of the story. She stopped for awhile to regain her composure. She told me that, instinctively, she knew that she had to lie still. She heard two men yelling at each other about shovels. The dead bodies needed to be covered but they could not find the shovels. They realized that the shovels must have been left at the bottom of the pit and decided to return to town to get more.

She knew this was her chance. When the two men left, it was eerily quiet. Jana remarked, "It is still beyond my comprehension how I found the strength to get out from the hole, covered as I was in dead bodies that were still warm." Clearly, a person's desire to live is a very strong instinct.

At this point, I interrupted Jana to ask how she got the scar on her forehead. She said that when she finally managed to get out of the hole, she stood up but was trembling and fell, hitting her head on the edge of a chainsaw. As her head bled, she ran as fast as she could. She found her way out of the woods and continued to run along the side of the road. It was very dark and she was hysterical. A girl of her age should never have been in such a situation.

Eventually, Jana stopped in front of the first house at the edge of town. She was covered in blood and remembered thinking that she didn't know the people who lived there. A dog started barking, which brought a man from the house. He took one look at Jana and gathered her into his arms. She felt safe and comfortable, falling asleep as he held her.

The husband and wife who saved her were "heavenly angels," she said. They lived modestly, but shared all they had with her. Their pure human instincts dictated that this little girl had to survive the evils of that time. They didn't have children of their own. As time passed, Jana recovered and grew close to the couple. They became her foster parents and helped her to survive the war. Her own parents never returned.

She confided to me that the horrors she had experienced had left her shattered. For most of her adult life, Jana had required medication to help her function. I sensed that she needed to finally reveal her story and I felt privileged to be the first to hear it and hoped that she would now be freed from this burden. When we parted, Jana felt it had been a very successful holiday. I was glad. Feeling better is what holidays are all about.

In later years, when discussing Jana's story with my family, I felt there was no other way to view it – Jana's survival was a miracle.

～

Many years after the war, in 1963, I had an opportunity to repay the Rokovs – the couple who had hidden me in their wine cellar during

that precarious time of deportation – for their kindness. I wasn't looking for an opportunity to pay back old debts, but one presented itself
when our oldest child, Tamara, was in her last year of high school.

At this stage in their academic lives, my daughter and her fellow
students were focused on final exams and seeking admission to university. It was a stressful time for them, and for their families too.
Throughout my children's school years I gladly spent time volun-
teering for the parents' association and I had been chosen to be the
parent representative of my daughter's graduating class. The position
involved sitting on various school committees, one of which had the
job of preparing references for students' admission to university. This
committee included the teachers of the graduating classes, the principal, a representative of the board of education, the school secretary of
the Communist Party, school union representatives, and the parent
representative of each of the four graduating classes.

It was not a pleasant job. It meant participating in decision-
making about students with whom, in some cases, I wasn't familiar.
When cases were simple and straight-forward I nodded my head af-
firmatively. Sometimes, however, the situations were not so clear-cut.
For example, we not only discussed the student's grades, but also the
family's background and their political leanings. We were to review
each family's activities during the war and determine whether or not
their background was "bourgeois," what their political associations
were after the war, and other personal matters.

Without a doubt, the parents' social standing in the past was the
most crucial criteria. The communist regime placed great importance
on belonging to the "correct" social class. If a family had a middle-class
background, if they had owned a house or other real estate, or if they
were successful in business, it spelled disaster from the committee's
perspective. The closer a family was to a working-class background
meant that the student had a greater chance in being recommended
to university, notwithstanding academic achievements. Moreover, if
there were family members with known criminal war activities, the

committee would not look favourably upon the student. Since few families could claim a true working-class background and a squeaky clean record during the war, most families tried not to advertise their past. The best possible thing for a student, aside from good grades, was if his or her parents were members of the Communist Party. In an attempt to give students a fair chance, the committee reviewed and weighed all of the facts and, when necessary, tried to put the information in the best light possible.

One day, I was surprised to receive a phone call from the daughter of the couple who had hidden me in their wine cellar. As far as I knew, she was still unaware of how her parents had helped me. Prior to her phone call, we had met once or twice on the streets of Bratislava, where she too had moved, chatted briefly and then parted. Now, during our phone conversation, she invited me for a visit, mentioning that our children were classmates. I hadn't been aware of that, as her son was known by her husband's last name and they weren't involved in the parents' association. She was especially pleasant to me, which I attributed to her probable fear that her husband's fascist political membership during the war might emerge and hurt their son's chance of being accepted to a university. At that time, many people worried that unfortunate information about their activities during the war might slip out of the mouths of old acquaintances. The reason for her invitation was immediately clear: she needed my help.

Members of the committee weren't permitted to review students' files privately, but I knew that the son's marks were not high and that his parents' background would be another obstacle. There was nothing I could do until his case was presented. In the interim, we spoke on the telephone a few times. I knew for certain that I would not hesitate to support a positive reference for the boy.

When the time came, I forthrightly expressed my conviction that the young man's attitude to studying would improve and that he would prove to be an asset to the school. His marks, although only average, indicated that he was not a lost cause. And regarding the father's political past, I pointed out that he had been an inactive member of the Hlinka Party and that he had registered only in an attempt to procure a position as a lawyer. I also spoke highly of the family's background, expressing my wish that more families had been as admirable as this one had been. I recommended highly that the committee support his request to be admitted to the university of his choice.

As a result of my efforts, the Rokovs' grandson received a positive recommendation for his application to medical school. The committee remained unaware of the debt I had repaid.

~

In Bratislava, we continued to make new friends and we were always glad when we reunited with old ones too. One of the old friends we met up with was Martin Ladder. The Ladder family had had deep roots in Humenné, and Martin was the eldest surviving son. He was married with two children and enjoyed a high position in the provincial government at the ministry of agriculture – the Povereníctvo poľnohospodárstva. His younger brother had settled in Prague, the capital city, approximately four hundred kilometres away. Their only surviving sister had moved with her husband to the most eastern part of the country and lived a very quiet life.

Before the war, the Ladder family had been well-established, affluent and part of the higher echelons of Jewish society. They had owned a house on the most prominent part of Main Street. The family of eight lived upstairs and their textile store was below. In the early 1920s their textile business had been prosperous but the Depression had taken its toll and they never totally recovered. The family hid their financial problems well for a time; however, the profits from the business were not sufficient to cover the cost and lifestyle of such a sizable family. Times were tough for all, but especially for Jews. Omens of our unprecedented future were everywhere.

By the 1930s some of the Ladder children were adults, but the three youngest were still in their teens. The oldest Ladder daughter,

Bella, was still unmarried in her thirties. She was considered good-looking and intelligent, not to mention kind and well-mannered. Her family wanted to find her a suitable match and when, finally, a widower with two little girls came on the scene, they were pleased. He was a well-to-do businessman who had suddenly lost his young wife to an illness. Everyone agreed that this alliance would be attractive for both parties – an old established family uniting with new money. As usual, a dowry was expected. The Ladders had decided long before the engagement that their piano, the pride of their household, would go to their eldest daughter. It represented so much to them – their earlier life of wealth and culture.

The newlyweds' neighbours enjoyed listening to the lovely music that emanated from the family's open windows. They all came to look forward to listening to the bride's afternoon recitals. After a while the neighbours noticed that the piano was being played less frequently. They soon found out it was because Bella was expecting, and she was suffering through a difficult pregnancy. Eventually Bella had a girl and the happy family busily tended to the new infant, whose navy-blue baby carriage was now a feature on Main Street. But while Bella was enjoying her new family, the war and the persecution and genocide of the Jews was intensifying. Before long, the whole extended family left Hummené and went into hiding together. Our paths went in different directions as we all fought for our survival, and I lost track of them.

After the war, when the survivors started to gather in our native town to share both horrible stories and miracles, I heard the fate of the Ladder clan. The whole extended family – with the exception of three siblings who had run away to other parts of Slovakia – perished in a merciless German bombardment while waiting for a train at a station filled with civilians. Apparently, everyone there was killed. I also heard that someone saw pieces of a navy-blue baby carriage all over the station.

I never found out who kept the piano during the war, or how it ended up in Martin Ladder's apartment in Bratislava. When I saw the piano it was in perfect condition. It was unscathed from the war, as if it had emerged from a peaceful world. Majestic as always, it was covered with a huge petite-pointe cover. It was a beautiful enhancement to his living room.

In the early 1950s, I learned that Martin's family was being unexpectedly transferred to the eastern part of the country. We speculated about the possible reason behind this transfer, but one thing was certain – this move was not voluntary. Martin's wife approached me, explaining that the other Ladder siblings had shown no interest in having the piano. Perhaps it reminded them too much of the past or maybe it was simply about the logistics or the complications regarding moving a piano. At any rate, the piano was offered to us until the Ladder family decided they were ready to take it back. It was moved into our home where our children used it for the following fifteen years that we remained in Slovakia. It became one of our prized possessions, even though it was not ours to keep.

Our children still remember the piano from their childhood and I can still see it clearly, standing in the corner of our sizable living room in Bratislava, facing the window. It was an imposing piece, a baby grand made of highly lacquered ebony. The piano was made by Förster, which at that time was the best make from that part of Europe. Over the years, the piano needed professional tuning only once. We tried not to think about the fact that the regal instrument did not really belong to us, that we had only temporary custody of it. We didn't know how long we would be allowed to keep it and never dared to ask. Eventually, we came to take its presence for granted, as if it were truly ours.

On August 20, 1968, the Soviets occupied Czechoslovakia. When the tanks rolled in, we decided to leave the country where the graves of our ancestors lay, the country of our birth. It was time to pack our belongings and flee once again. We would have to leave all of our belongings behind, which of course included the piano. When the time came to part with it, it felt as if we were leaving behind a cherished family member. The music made on it had a significant role in our children's lives, as it must also have touched the lives of those who had owned it. I worried about who would look after its shiny surface and keep the ivory keys clean. I had no choice but to close the doors and not look back.

Later, in Canada, I often thought about our old piano and wondered what had become of it. Eventually, I found out that a family had settled into our fully furnished apartment where the piano remained. Leaving the piano behind and ultimately losing it to strangers was, for me, a tremendous loss. The times in Czechoslovakia continued to be unstable and after a couple of years the family reportedly moved out and left the apartment empty. They were gone without a trace, along with our beloved piano. I will probably never know if it still exists and whose lives it is having an impact on now.

Life in Canada

Until 1968 we lived and brought up our four children under a Communist regime. The system discouraged self-identifying according to race, ethnicity or religion, so it wasn't advisable to stand tall and proud with regard to our Jewish heritage; still, we hadn't hidden it. Our children always knew who they were, but we weren't observant and we didn't give them a Jewish education. Perhaps we could have, but we didn't want to take the risk of calling any undesired attention to our family. The best course was to not advertise our background. It was expected that we would be assimilated, which was part of an unwritten law.

In 1957, when my son Michael was around seven years old, he and his friend announced to their classmates that they were Jewish and instructed them to "keep it confidential." The other children had no idea what the two were talking about – the significance of this announcement was lost on them. Michael must have felt safe enough to share this information with his classmates, but understood that there was something secretive and unpopular about being Jewish.

In the fall of 1968, one week after the Soviets came to occupy Czechoslovakia, my family and Arthur's brothers and their families escaped to Vienna, the closest neighbouring free city. We left by train with only a few of our belongings, telling the ticket inspection agent that we were going on a short trip and would return. We arrived in

Vienna two weeks before Rosh Hashanah, the Jewish new year and the first of the high holy days. Not accustomed to attending synagogue, we chatted with friends in front of a Jewish community centre, near a synagogue with a full congregation. It was a sunny September day and many men were outside having a midday break. They all wore yarmulkes – small head coverings. Growing up in communist Czechoslovakia, my children saw neither hats nor yarmulkes on men attending synagogue. I clearly remember that day they first encountered Jews practicing their religion openly. Matthew, my youngest child, who was almost fifteen at the time, watched the men intently and then expressed surprise at how many bald men there were with covered heads! He had no idea that the men wore the head coverings out of respect for God and not to hide their baldness.

We were in Vienna for about six weeks and deciding where to go from there was difficult. One thing we knew for sure: Arthur and his brothers, wherever we went, wanted to stay together. After their horrible experiences of terror and separation, they had all remained close. After discussing where we knew people, we decided that we would go to Canada and build a new life in a democratic country. Canada's doors were open to refugees from Czechoslovakia – between 1968 and 1969, approximately 21,000 Czechs and Slovaks immigrated to Canada.

We arrived in Toronto on October 24, 1968. As newcomers, we experienced many initial difficulties and it was years before we felt truly settled. We adopted Canada as our homeland and hoped this new land would view us as loyal citizens. I remember many times returning to Toronto from visits elsewhere and experiencing a warm feeling when I recognized the skyline of the city from a distance. Yes, this was our city; it was good to come home.

Our first few years were busy as we built our new lives. It had been the right decision to leave the old country, where the people were bending under the "friendly" occupation of the Soviet army. I went to school for bookkeeping for one year and then got an accounting job at Jutan International, where I worked for about twen-ty-three years. Arthur worked in the water resources department for the Ontario Ministry of the Environment. My life was divided between family and work. Our extended family was together and we were content. Eventually, our original family of six grew, thank God, to eighteen!

In Canada, what it meant to be Jewish became clearer to our children. Although we could practice our Judaism openly, as my fa-ther had before the Nazis invaded, customs were different in North America than they had been during my father's lifetime in Slovakia. For example, my father, who was an observant Jew and lived accord-ing to *halacha* (Jewish law) his whole life, never owned or wore a yarmulke. Instead he always kept a hat on while in synagogue. Here in North America I saw mostly yarmulkes, not hats, on men in synagogue.

To varying degrees, all of our children studied Judaism as adults and are passing the traditions on to their own children. In 1996, al-most forty years after Michael announced that he was Jewish to his classmates in Bratislava, Arthur and I visited him and his family in Connecticut for my grandson David's bar mitzvah. We are always happy to spend time with our children and their families and are proud to see how well they are all doing.

On this visit, of course, we were all focused on the upcoming bar mitzvah. My son was very excited to have come up with the idea of using what he referred to as "our" Torah scroll for the service. What did he mean by "our" Torah we asked? To our amazement, we were shown a Torah with a lilac velvet cover and on the end of one of the wooden handles was a plaque that read: No. 207, Czech Memorial Scrolls, Westminster Synagogue, London UK 1964–5724. I had never heard about the Czech scrolls before this.

Michael told us the story, which had begun more than fifty years earlier, in the days of the Protectorate of Bohemia and Moravia – the part of Czechoslovakia annexed by Nazi Germany. In 1942, when the

Nazis were on top of the world and began erasing Jewish existence, they began collecting confiscated religious items to be housed in the Jewish Museum in Prague for a permanent exhibition of Jewish life. These relics would be the remainders of an extinct race. They collected more than fifteen hundred Torah scrolls, some more than one hundred years old.

After the war, the scrolls were stacked in an unused synagogue in Prague, where they lay deteriorating until 1964. A group of philanthropic British Jews found out about the scrolls and had them moved to the Westminster Synagogue in London. Here the Torahs were repaired as much as possible and distributed to synagogues and Jewish organizations around the world.

In 1988, one of these scrolls made its way to Temple Israel in Waterbury, Connecticut. Scroll No. 207 was from the town of Uhlířské Janovice. Members of the temple felt privileged to provide a home and to care for the Torah. It was used to commemorate special occasions. Sometime later, Temple Israel closed and the Czech scroll was given to Michael for safekeeping. It was still in his care when the time came for my grandson David's bar mitzvah. How appropriate, we all agreed, that he would read his portion from this scroll.

Having the Czech scroll was very meaningful for Michael and his family, and for all of us it is another symbol of our survival and the continuation of our heritage. The Torah is a precious possession to the Jews. It is a connection to the people of ancient times. These precious symbols of our faith had been piled in a heap, awaiting a display that was to testify to our demise. Now we could celebrate the survival of our people and heritage.

The days when our Judaism could not be advertised are now far behind us. In North America, my family enjoys the freedom to live a spiritual life openly. We are free to be who we are. In spite of their minimal Jewish upbringing, it was natural for our children to continue the legacy of Judaism. As my mother used to say, "Blood is thicker than water."

So much time has passed since our arrival in Canada. Arthur, Eman and Victor have enjoyed their retirement years together. We have all lived in the same city and have watched each other's families grow. The Sermer brothers share a special relationship that has lasted a lifetime, and I am proud to be a part of their family.

Reflections

I paint sometimes and, when trying to express happiness, I will typically choose pastel shades of pink, white or yellow – colours that, to me, represent the innocence of youth, the rebirth of nature in the spring and the dawning of a new day. How we use and respond to colour fascinates me. For me, as for many people, each colour has a meaning associated with it. Seeing things through a lens of brightness is a reflection of my positive outlook on life. But when I am having a grey day, I rarely can be found in front of my easel.

I once attended the debut exhibit of a young Slovak artist and recognized the dark emotions his paintings represented. Something about his work both riveted and disturbed me. The abstract dark lines that ambled vertically, horizontally and in circles across one canvas fascinated me. Two of the paintings gave the impression of the same two people facing each other, each viewed from a different angle. I was troubled by the pictures but did not understand the full meaning of them until I noticed the description provided nearby. The young artist was a child of victims of the Holocaust. He was alone, missing his family and haunted by memories of his childhood. His use of colour reflected his state of mind – dark equalled night and night meant dreams, dreams that must have been filled with sickening images.

Over the course of the next decade I followed the artist's development, viewing his work at exhibits from time to time. As the years went by, I noticed that his later work left me with a different impression than the earlier paintings. Changes in his life and emotions were reflected in a steady increase in the use of brighter colours. It seemed obvious to me that with the passing of time he found more positive meaning in his life. When I looked at his paintings many years after the first exhibit, I felt that he had arrived and anchored in a brighter port, where he hopefully experienced quiet happiness and satisfaction. Like me, he was a survivor.

And yet, lately I find myself asking if those dark images still remain. "Is the world a jungle or a zoo?" I ask myself. I feel as though I have lived in both. Perhaps all of us have. The peaceful animals that God created, living free in the jungle, have an instinct for self-preservation that may protect them from predators. How else could they survive? I suppose it's the natural order of things that when beasts prey on other animals, they ensure a balanced population of creatures.

Does human society mirror animal life in the jungle? No, I don't think human nature was meant to be so cruel. Even in the animal world, predators do not kill out of vengeance or hate – they prey on other creatures to ensure their own survival.

I think that living under Soviet-style communism in Eastern Europe was similar to living in a zoo. Living under the communist regime, people were captives, although safe from many of the ravages of jungle life. But that ideology, which sounded so humane, was a fallacy. Communism was born with bloodshed into a weak and unprepared society. It struggled throughout its whole life, fed with fanfare, until it reached the moment when it abruptly stopped breathing. Behind the bars of communism, there were countless lives that ended prematurely.

Not long ago, on a late September day, I went strolling in a nearby park in Toronto. Between the large trees flowed a creek that had sections of it reshaped by groundskeepers in order to help the wildlife move more freely. Ducks and geese enjoyed the environment and the free meals provided by visiting adults and children. The birds had a secure life in the park and, not surprisingly, refused to migrate south that winter. They had come to expect to be fed and had forgotten how to live the way nature intended. As a result of this dependence, the birds froze in the cold.

Just like those animals were fooled, so too do protected systems often fool us. If we are not to freeze in the cold, we have to be able to take care of ourselves, even if it is a struggle. Those of us who survived under both the Nazi and communist regimes would prefer to live in freedom, even if life is not easy. The natural order of things teaches us to fend for ourselves. Inhabitants of a zoo may be safe, but they are helpless captives without the richness that makes life worth living.

I believe that most ideologies and movements known to human-kind have specific places in history. They lived a certain length of time, fulfilled their purpose, and in one way or another disappeared from the world scene. Zionism, though, seems to have outlived them all. For centuries, Jews have been committed to establishing a Jewish state in the Land of Israel. What makes Zionism unique? Zionism was nurtured over thousands of years by a people whose own history has mirrored that of the movement's – a history that involved creation, destruction and a stubborn perseverance that enabled it to survive. Zionism is a movement based on a promise made by God to the Jewish people and I don't underestimate the strength that this gives to the ideology.

Perhaps this is why the Jewish people have survived at all. The Jewish people were born out of a promise made by God and have managed thus far to live through both prosperous times of growth and health, and treacherous times of exile and oppression. What does the future hold for us? Of course we can't know. Yet I have faith that we will neither live a mere predator-prey lifestyle nor the captive life of zoo animals. Courage, wisdom and a few miracles will ensure our survival and shape our destiny.

Epilogue

Excerpt from a dvar torah delivered by my granddaughter Becky Sermer at her bat mitzvah on June 23, 2001.

I began studying for my bat mitzvah like everyone does – learning about my Torah and Haftorah portions and trying to figure out what lessons I could learn from them. But along the way, I was also learning about my own family. I realized that there was a connection between the two. Each tells the story about how families take care of their members and provide for the next generation.

My Torah portion, Chukat, takes place towards the end of the Israelites' forty years of wandering in the desert after they left Egypt. The people were led by Moses, his brother Aaron and their sister Miriam. One of Miriam's important roles had been finding drinking water in wells throughout the desert. At the beginning of the portion she died, and as a result the people were desperate for water. They complained to Moses and Aaron, who went to God for guidance. God told Moses to order a rock to give water. Frustrated with the Israelites' complaining, Moses lost his temper and in anger struck the rock instead. Water poured out of the rock. God punished Moses and Aaron by not allowing them to go with their people into the Land of Israel. Before reaching the Promised Land, Aaron and Moses would also die. None of the three leaders ever actually got to share the full victory and celebration with their people.

As I was studying my portion, I realized that even though Miriam was a very important leader, her death was only mentioned in one short sentence. The rest of the portion goes on to explain the details of what happens to Moses, Aaron and the people of Israel. I also learned that Miriam is only mentioned eleven times in the whole Torah, compared to hundreds of times that Moses and Aaron are mentioned. This puzzled me because I know that the Israelites probably could not have survived without Miriam. I couldn't understand why losing her seemed to be treated so casually in the Torah. I wondered if it was because men wrote the Torah that they told mostly stories about men. We never really got to hear many details about Miriam and the other women.

While I was studying my Torah and Haftorah portions, I was also reading two works written by my two grandmothers. They each lived through the Holocaust and a few years ago they wrote about their experiences during the war. It was hard to believe what horrible conditions they lived in and what terrifying situations they had to face. I learned so much that I never knew about them – how brave they were and how strong they had been to survive. I feel very sad thinking about my grandmothers being young and dealing with such horrifying experiences. I kept thinking that if I was in their situation, I could never have been as courageous as they were. Even though I wish they never had to go through those difficult times, I am proud to have grandmothers of such great strength and will to survive.

We never got to hear Miriam's story the way she would have told it; I am lucky that my grandmothers were able to tell their own stories about coming out of the Egypt of their time. I have benefited from their courage and their desire for something better for themselves and their family. My grandmother Zuzana wrote, "My aim is to enlighten those who want to listen and to share the thread of hope that has woven through my life, hope that has been based on how I perceive the world around me. My experiences have led me to believe though, that we must always be prepared to help ourselves. Thank

God, in most situations we are able to do so." My grandmother Halina ended her story by saying, "When I think of all the innocent children who perished for no reason, I think of my own beautiful children and grandchildren. And I am hopeful that they will live in a better world."

Because of Moses, Aaron and Miriam, the Israelites were safely led into the Promised Land. What the three leaders did was a brave sacrifice for their people. They never felt the joy of experiencing a life in the Land of Israel. My grandparents left their lives in Europe to give a hopeful future to their children and grandchildren. My grandfather Arthur was a successful scientist in Czechoslovakia when he brought his family to Canada. He sacrificed his career to let his children build theirs in a freer and better world. My grandparents put their families' needs first in their lives. My grandparents showed me that nothing is more important than family. I thank them for giving me constant encouragement, love and confidence. I see them as the leaders of our family who rescued not only themselves, but also our family's future.

Glossary

Agudath Israel (Hebrew; union of Israel) An Orthodox political organization established in 1912 that stood for elections in Poland. The direction of the party in religious, social and political issues was determined by Torah scholars. After World War I, the movement gained a foothold in Slovakia, where local Orthodox leaders realized that a worldwide organization was necessary to combat secular Zionist influences. Agudath Israel was founded in Slovakia in 1919 as a distinct and independent group from the worldwide Agudah movement. The Slovak organization opposed cooperation with other Jewish groups and was firmly rooted in traditional Jewish education from the Torah and Talmud. *See also* Orthodox.

aliyah (Hebrew; pl. *aliyot*, literally, ascent) A term used by Jews and modern Israelis to refer to Jewish immigration to Israel; the term is also used to refer to "going up" to the altar in a synagogue to read from the Torah.

antisemitism Prejudice, discrimination, persecution and/or hatred against Jewish people, institutions, culture and symbols.

arizátors (Slovak; Aryanizer) A non-Jewish person appointed to manage a business confiscated from a Jewish owner.

Arrow Cross Party (Hungarian; *Nyilaskeresztes Párt – Hungarista Mozgalom*; abbreviation: Nyilas) A Hungarian nationalistic and antisemitic party founded by Ferenc Szálasi in 1935 under the name the Party of National Will. With the full support of Nazi Germany, the newly renamed Arrow Cross Party ran in Hungary's 1939 election and won 25 per cent of the vote. The party was banned shortly after the elections, but was legalized again in March 1944 when Germany occupied Hungary. Under Nazi approval, the party assumed control of Hungary from October 15, 1944, to March 1945, led by Szálasi under the name the Government of National Unity. The Arrow Cross regime was particularly brutal toward Jews – they deported more than 70,000 to Nazi camps and murdered more than 10,000 during their short period of rule. *See also* Szálasi, Ferenc.

Auschwitz (German; in Polish, Oświęcim) A town in southern Poland approximately forty kilometres from Krakow, it is also the name of the largest complex of Nazi concentration camps that were built nearby. The Auschwitz complex contained three main camps: Auschwitz I, a slave labour camp built in May 1940; Auschwitz II-Birkenau, a death camp built in early 1942; and Auschwitz-Monowitz, a slave labour camp built in October 1942. In 1941 Auschwitz I was a testing site for usage of the lethal gas Zyklon B as a method of mass killing, which then went into wide usage. The Auschwitz complex was liberated by the Soviet army in January 1945.

Austro-Hungarian Empire Also known as the Dual Monarchy of Austria and Hungary, ruled by the royal Habsburg family. It was successor to the Austrian Empire (1804–1867) and functioned as a dual-union state in Central Europe from 1867 to 1918. A multinational empire, the Dual Monarchy was notable for the constant political and ethnic disputes among its eleven principal national groups. Although the Empire adopted a Law of Nationalities, which officially accorded language and cultural rights to various ethnic groups, in practice, there were many inequalities in how the groups were treated. Jews were granted both citizenship rights and equal status to other minority groups, but minorities such as the Slovaks, for example, were excluded from the political sphere, whereas Czechs were accepted into government positions. The Austro-Hungarian Empire dissolved at the end of World War I and divided into the separate and independent countries of Austria, Hungary and Czechoslovakia.

banderowcy (Ukrainian) The informal term for Ukrainian nationalist guerrillas led by Stepan Bandera under the auspices of the Organization of Ukrainian Nationalists (OUN) and its military wing, the Ukrainska Povstanska Armiya (UPA). Many of its members were antisemitic and led anti-Jewish pogroms after the war. The UPA was formally disbanded in 1949 but continued to have a localized presence until 1956.

bar mitzvah/bat mitzvah (Hebrew; literally, one to whom commandments apply) The age of thirteen when, according to Jewish tradition, boys become religiously and morally responsible for their actions and are considered adults for the purpose of synagogue ritual. A bar mitzvah is also the synagogue ceremony and family celebration that mark the attainment of this status, during which the boy is called upon to read a portion of the Torah and recite the prescribed prayers in a public prayer forum. In the latter half of the twentieth century, liberal Jews instituted an equivalent ceremony and celebration for girls – called a bat mitzvah.

Betar A Zionist youth movement founded by Revisionist Zionist leader Ze'ev Jabotinsky in 1923 that encouraged the development of a new generation of Zionist activists based on the ideals of courage, self-respect, military training, defence of Jewish life and property, and settlement in Israel to establish a Jewish state in British Mandate Palestine. During the 1930s and 1940s, as antisemitism increased and the Nazis launched their murderous campaign against the Jews of Europe, Betar rescued thousands of Jews by organizing illegal immigration to British Mandate Palestine. The Betar movement today, closely aligned with Israel's right-wing Likud party, remains involved in supporting Jewish and Zionist activism around the world.

Beth hamidrash (Hebrew) Study hall.

Beth Jacob (in Hebrew, Beit Yaakov; house of Jacob) A movement founded in Poland in 1917 by seamstress Sarah Schenirer (1883–1935) to provide formal Orthodox Jewish education for girls. Although her ideas about girls' education first met with ridicule and opposition, Schenirer's initiative was eventually recognized by the Agudath Israel movement in 1919 and fully endorsed by 1923. By the early 1930s, Beth Jacob schools were located in more than twenty cities and towns throughout Czechoslovakia, including Humenné, as well as all over Europe. *See also* Agudath Israel.

Blockälteste (German; literally, block elder) A prisoner appointed by the German authorities as barracks supervisor, charged with maintaining order and accorded certain privileges.

Bnei Akiva (Hebrew; children of Akiva) The youth wing of the Orthodox Mizrachi Zionist movement founded in British Mandate Palestine in 1929 and still in existence internationally today. Their philosophy is that *Torah*, or religious commitment, and *Avodah*, work, go hand in hand. The concept of *Avodah* was initially interpreted as agricultural work but today has a broader definition of work that helps Israel develop as a modern state. *See also* Mizrachi.

British Mandate Palestine The area of the Middle East under British rule from 1923 to 1948, as established by the League of Nations after World War I. During that time, the United Kingdom restricted Jewish immigration. The area currently encompasses present-day Israel, Jordan, the West Bank and the Gaza Strip.

Buda The western part of Budapest, situated west of the Danube River. The area comprises about one-third of Budapest and is mostly hilly and wooded. *See also* Pest.

Chukat (Hebrew; decree) The 39th weekly portion of the Torah, which is read in synagogue every year in June or July. *See also* Torah.

Dachau The Nazis' first concentration camp, which was established primarily to house political prisoners in March 1933. The Dachau camp was located about sixteen kilometres northwest of Munich in southern Germany. The number of Jews interned there rose considerably after Kristallnacht pogroms on the night of November 9–10, 1938. In 1942 a crematorium area was constructed next to the main camp. By the spring of 1945, Dachau and its subcamps held more than 67,665 registered prisoners – 43,350 categorized as political prisoners and 22,100 as Jews. As the American Allied forces neared the camp in April 1945, the Nazis forced 7,000 prisoners, primarily Jews, on a gruelling death march to Tegernsee, another camp in southern Germany.

gendarmes Members of a military or paramilitary force.

Gestapo (German) Short for Geheime Staatspolizei, the Secret State Police of Nazi Germany. The Gestapo was the brutal force that dealt with the perceived enemies of the Nazi regime and were responsible for rounding up European Jews for deportation to the death camps. They operated with very few legal constraints and were also responsible for issuing exit visas to the residents of German-occupied areas. A number of Gestapo members also joined the Einsatzgruppen, the mobile killing squads responsible for the roundup and murder of Jews in eastern Poland and the USSR through mass shooting operations.

ghetto A confined residential area for Jews. The term originated in Venice, Italy in 1516 with a law requiring all Jews to live on a segregated, gated island known as Ghetto Nuovo. Throughout the Middle Ages in Europe, Jews were often forcibly confined to gated Jewish neighbourhoods. During the Holocaust, the Nazis forced Jews to live in crowded and unsanitary conditions in rundown districts of cities and towns.

hachshara (Hebrew; literally, preparation) A training program to prepare new immigrants for life in the Land of Israel.

Häftling (German) Prison inmate.

Haftorah The portion read from the Book of Prophets after the Torah reading at Sabbath services and major festivals; it is traditionally sung by the youth who is celebrating his or her bar/bat mitzvah. *See also* Torah.

Hashomer Hatzair (Hebrew) The Youth Guard. A left-wing Zionist youth movement founded in Central Europe in the early twentieth century to prepare young Jews to become workers and farmers, to establish kibbutzim – collective settlements – in pre-state Israel and work the land as pioneers. Before World War II, there were 70,000 Hashomer Hatzair members worldwide and many of those in Nazi-occupied territories led resistance activities in the ghettos and concentration camps or joined partisan groups in the forests of east-central Europe. It is the oldest Zionist youth movement still in existence. *See also* Betar, Bnei Akiva; Zionism.

Hasidism (from the Hebrew word *hasid*; literally, piety) An Orthodox Jewish spiritual movement founded by Rabbi Israel ben Eliezer in eighteenth-century Poland; characterized by philosophies of mysticism and focusing on joyful prayer. This movement resulted in a new kind of leader who attracted disciples as opposed to the traditional rabbis who focused on the intellectual study of Jewish law. Melody and dance have an important role in Hasidic worship. There are many different sects of Hasidic Judaism, but followers of Hasidism often wear dark, conservative clothes as well as a head covering to reflect modesty and show respect to God.

high holidays (also High Holy Days) The autumn holidays that mark the beginning of the Jewish year and that include Rosh Hashanah (New Year) and Yom Kippur (Day of Atonement). Rosh Hashanah is observed by synagogue services where the leader of the service blows the shofar (ram's horn), and festive meals where sweet foods, such as apples and honey, are eaten to symbolize and celebrate a sweet new year. Yom Kippur, a day of fasting and prayer at synagogue, follows ten days later.

Hlinka's Slovak People's Party Named for its founder and first chairman, Father Andrej Hlinka, the HSSP was a strongly nationalist, Catholic, totalitarian and antisemitic party that became the first government of the newly autonomous Slovak Republic in 1939. Its wartime president, who had taken over as chairman of the HSSP after Hlinka's death in 1938, was Catholic priest Jozef Tiso. The Hlinka Guard, the fascist, paramilitary wing of the new autonomous Slovak regime, was established in October 1938.

Ilava A town in western Slovakia that was the site of a labour/internment camp during World War II.

International Brigades The general name for the military units that volunteered from more than fifty countries to travel to Spain and support the Spanish Republic by fighting against the fascist Nationalist forces during the Spanish Civil War. Approximately 60,000 volunteers, of which 1,000 were from Hungary, held either combative or non-combative roles between 1936 and 1939. *See also* Spanish Civil War.

Internationale A well-known and widely sung left-wing anthem. Adopted by the socialist movement in the late 19th century, it was the de facto national anthem of the Soviet Union until 1944, and is still sung by left-wing groups to this day.

Jewish Code Anti-Jewish legislation modelled after the Nuremberg Laws that was passed in Slovakia on September 9, 1941. A subsequent measure to the antisemitic laws that began in 1939, which dismissed Jews from the government and military, and the 1940 Aryanization Acts that expropriated property, the code contained an additional 270 measures, including one ordering Jews to wear a yellow Star of David for identification. *See also* Nuremberg Laws.

Judenrat (German; pl. *Judenräte*) Jewish Council. A group of Jewish leaders appointed by the Germans to administer and provide services to the local Jewish population under occupation and carry out German orders. The *Judenräte* appeared to be self-governing entities, but were under complete German control. The *Judenräte* faced difficult and complex moral decisions under brutal conditions and remain a contentious subject. The chairmen had to decide whether to comply or refuse to comply with German demands. Some were killed by the Nazis for refusing, while others committed suicide. Jewish officials who advocated compliance thought that cooperation might save at least some Jews. Some who denounced resistance efforts did so because they believed that armed resistance would bring death to the entire community.

KEOKH (Külföldieket Ellenorzo Országos Központi Hivatal) National Central Alien Control Office. A Hungarian bureau created in 1930 that dealt with permits for refugees and other foreign citizens and is still in existence today.

Kremnička A village in central Slovakia where members of the resistance involved in the Slovak National Uprising, as well as women and children, were murdered and buried in a mass grave in November 1944. In 1949, a memorial was placed there for the 747 victims of the massacre that mentioned various ethnicities but negated Jewish victims. In 1995, the memorial was adjusted to commemorate Jewish victims by adding a menorah inscribed with the Hebrew word *Zakhor* (remember). *See also* Slovak National Uprising.

Manfred Weiss Works Hungary's largest armaments and machinery industrial complex during World War II. In 1944, the company was owned by the interrelated Chorin and Weiss families, who entered into negotiations with SS officer Kurt Becher for control of the company in exchange for their families' lives. Although there were legal roadblocks to the SS acquiring a company under Hungarian control – mostly because the firm was partially owned by non-Jews – and it countered Germany's agreement about nominal Hungarian independence, the deal was eventually signed in May 1944. The SS acquired control of the company as a trusteeship in exchange for the lives of about fifty family members, who were granted safe passage out of Hungary to Portugal and Switzerland, and were also paid approximately $600,000. *See also* SS.

Masaryk, Tomáš G. (1850–1937) Founder and first president of Czechoslovakia. He was known for his strong public opposition to antisemitism. *See also* Polná Affair.

minyan (Hebrew) The quorum of ten adult male Jews required for certain religious rites. The term can also designate a congregation.

Mizrachi (acronym of Merkaz Ruchani; Hebrew, spiritual centre) An Orthodox nationalist Zionist movement founded in Vilna, Lithuania in 1902. Mizrachi was founded on the belief that the Torah is central to Zionism and Jewish life. The movement's principles are encompassed in its slogan "The land of Israel for the people of Israel according to the Torah of Israel." *See also* Bnei Akiva; Zionism.

Nuremberg Laws The September 1935 laws that stripped Jews of their civil rights as German citizens and separated them from Germans legally, socially and politically. They were first announced at the Nazi party rally in the German city of Nuremberg in 1933. Under "The Law for the Protection of German Blood and Honor" Jews were defined as a separate race rather than a religious group; whether a person was racially Jewish was determined by ancestry (how many Jewish grandparents a person had). Among other things, the law forbade marriages or sexual relations between Jews and Germans. *See also* Jewish Code.

Nuremberg Trials A series of war crimes trials held in the city of Nuremberg between November 1945 and October 1946 that tried twenty-four key leaders of the Holocaust. A subsequent twelve trials, the Trials of War Criminals before the Nuremberg Military Tribunals, was held for lesser war criminals between December 1946 and April 1949.

Nyilas *See* Arrow Cross Party.

Orthodox Judaism The set of beliefs and practices of Jews for whom the observance of Jewish law is closely connected to faith; it is characterized by strict religious observance of Jewish dietary laws, restrictions on work on the Sabbath and holidays, and a modest code of dress.

partisans Members of irregular military forces or resistance movements formed to oppose armies of occupation. During World War II there were a number of different partisan groups that opposed both the Nazis and their collaborators in several countries. The term partisan could include highly organized, almost paramilitary groups such as the Red Army partisans; ad hoc groups bent more on survival than resistance; and roving groups of bandits who plundered what they could from all sides during the war.

Passover One of the major festivals of the Jewish calendar, Passover takes place over eight days in the spring. One of the main observances of the holiday is to recount the story of Exodus, the Jews' flight from slavery in Egypt, at a ritual meal called a seder. The name itself refers to the fact that God "passed over" the houses of the Jews when he set about slaying the firstborn sons of Egypt as the last of the ten plagues aimed at convincing Pharaoh to free the Jews.

Pest The mostly flat, commercial, eastern part of Budapest divided from Buda by the Danube River. It comprises about two-thirds of the city. *See also* Buda.

Polná Affair Also known as the Hilsner Affair. A series of antisemitic trials that took place in Bohemia against Leopold Hilsner, a poor Jew and drifter accused of murdering a Catholic girl, Anežka Hrůzová, in 1899 near the village of Polná. Although there was no evidence to support the accusation against him, Hilsner was convicted of this crime as well as – again with no evidence – the death of another girl two years earlier, whose manner of death could not be proven at all. Hilsner was first sentenced to death, which was later reduced to life imprisonment with the help of Tomáš Masaryk. Hilsner was eventually pardoned after spending ten years in prison. The Hilsner case was one of many trials fuelled by antisemitism at the time under the preposterous guise of the blood libel, the false accusation that Jews use the blood of Christian children to prepare matzah for Passover. *See also* Masaryk, Tomáš G.

razzia (German; raid) A term used during the Nazi regime to refer to a roundup of people for forced labour, deportation or mass killing.

Roma Also known as Romani. An ethnic group primarily located in central and eastern Europe. The Roma were commonly referred to as Gypsies in the past, a term now generally considered to be derogatory, and they have often been subject to persecution. During the Holocaust, which the Roma refer to in Romani as the *Porajmos* – the devouring – they were stripped of their citizenship under the Nuremberg Laws and were targeted for death under Hitler's race policies. The estimation of how many Roma were killed varies widely and has been difficult to document – estimations generally range from between 200,000 to 1,000,000. *See also* Nuremberg Laws.

Roosevelt, Franklin D (1882–1945) President of the United States between 1933 and 1945. Although Roosevelt publically opposed Nazi Germany's treatment of German Jews, his government did not actively pursue an immigration policy that would welcome Jewish refugees – the US even went so far as to turn away the *St. Louis*, a ship that carried almost one thousand German Jews seeking asylum in 1939. Roosevelt was aware of the Nazis' murderous policies against Jews as early as 1942, but the US did not help rescue European Jews until January 1944 through the establishment of the War Refugee Board. In June 1944, after the Swiss press published excerpts of a report that detailed the Nazi atrocities against the Jews, Roosevelt joined the escalating international pressure on Hungary to stop the deportations of its Jewish citizens.

Rusyn An East Slavic language spoken in southwest Ukraine, northeast Slovakia, southeast Poland and Hungary.

Sabbath (Shabbat; Hebrew; in Yiddish, Shabbes, Shabbos) The weekly day of rest beginning Friday at sunset and ending Saturday at sundown ushered in by the lighting of candles on Friday night and the recitation of blessings over wine and challah (egg bread); a day of celebration as well as prayer, it is customary to eat three festive meals, attend synagogue services and refrain from doing any work or travelling.

scarlet fever A bacterial disease that caused a high mortality rate until the 1940s, when the common use of the penicillin antibiotic began treating it successfully.

shiva (Hebrew; literally, seven) In Judaism, the seven-day mourning period that is observed after the funeral of a close relative.

shtiebl (Yiddish; little house or little room) A small, unadorned prayer room or prayer house furnished like synagogues but much more modestly. Most observant Jews in Eastern Europe prayed in *shtiebls* on a daily basis; they attended services in a synagogue on holidays or sometimes on the Sabbath. *See also* Sabbath.

shul (Yiddish) Synagogue or Jewish house of prayer.

Slovak National Uprising (August 29, 1944–October 28, 1944) The anti-fascist armed resistance mounted against the pro-Nazi Slovak government by partisans in central Slovakia. The uprising, comprised of approximately 80,000 partisans from more than thirty countries, was poorly planned and was crushed by German forces in two months, although battles continued in the area until the end of the war. An estimated 85,000 casualties resulted from the uprising, and Nazi troops destroyed ninety-three Slovak villages in retaliation for their suspected cooperation with partisan forces. *See also* Kremnička.

Social Democratic Party (Hungary) (in Hungarian, *"történelmi" Szo-ciáldemokrata Párt*, s z d p) A socialist political party first formed in Austro-Hungary in 1890 that was previously known as The General Workers Association. The party was declared illegal after the Nazi occupation of Hungary in March 1944; many leaders were executed or imprisoned. Some members continued to operate underground until the war ended, when the party was once again legalized.

Spanish Civil War (1936–1939) The war in Spain between the military – supported by Conservative, Catholic and fascist elements, together called the Nationalists – and the democratically elected Republican government. Sparked by an initial coup that failed to win a decisive victory, the country was plunged into a bloody civil war. It ended when the Nationalists, under the leadership of General Francisco Franco, marched into Madrid. During the civil war, the Nationalists received aid from both Fascist Italy and Nazi Germany, and the Republicans received aid from volunteers worldwide. *See also* International Brigades.

SS Abbreviation for Schutzstaffel (Defence Corps). The SS was established in 1925 as Adolf Hitler's elite corps of personal bodyguards. Under the direction of Heinrich Himmler, its membership grew from 280 in 1929 to 50,000 when the Nazis came to power in 1933, and to nearly a quarter of a million on the eve of World War II. The SS was comprised of the Allgemeine-SS (General SS) and the Waffen-SS (Armed, or Combat SS). The General SS dealt with policing and the enforcement of Nazi racial policies in Germany and the Nazi-occupied countries. An important unit within the SS was the Reichssicherheitshauptamt (RSHA, the Central Office of Reich Security), whose responsibility included the Gestapo (Geheime Staatspolizei). The SS ran the concentration and death camps, with all their associated economic enterprises, and also fielded its own Waffen-SS military divisions, including some recruited from the occupied countries. *See also* Gestapo.

Szálasi, Ferenc (1897–1946) The founder and leader of the Hungarian fascist Arrow Cross Party that actively collaborated with the Nazis in Hungary, notably in the persecution and deportation of Jews. He was convicted of war crimes and executed in 1946. *See also* Arrow Cross Party.

tallis (Yiddish; in Hebrew, *tallit*) Jewish prayer shawl traditionally worn during morning prayers and on the Day of Atonement (Yom Kippur). One usually wears the *tallis* over one's shoulders but some choose to place it over their heads to express awe in the presence of God.

Talmud (Hebrew; literally, instruction or learning) An ancient rabbinic text that discusses Jewish history, law and ethics; it is comprised of two sections: the Mishnah, which is further subdivided into six sections and focuses on legal issues, and the Gemara, which analyzes the legal issues. *See also* Torah.

tefillin (Hebrew) Phylacteries. A pair of black leather boxes containing scrolls of parchment inscribed with bible verses and worn by Jews on the arm and forehead at prescribed times of prayer as a symbol of the covenantal relationship with God.

Tito, Josip Broz (1892–1980) The commander of the Yugoslav Partisans between 1941 and 1945 and president of Yugoslavia between 1953 and 1980. During World War II, Tito sided with the Allies and led an anti-fascist resistance movement that comprised various ethnicities, including Jews.

Torah (Hebrew) The Five Books of Moses (the first five books in the Bible), also called the Pentateuch. The Torah is the core of Jewish scripture, traditionally believed to have been given to Moses on Mount Sinai. In Christianity it is referred to as the "Old Testament." *See also* Talmud.

Treaty of Trianon One of the five treaties produced at the 1919 Paris Peace Conference organized by the victors of World War I. The Treaty of Trianon imposed a harsh peace on Hungary, exacting reparations and redrawing its borders so that Hungary lost over two-thirds of its territory and about two-thirds of its inhabitants.

treif (Yiddish) Food that is not allowed under Jewish dietary laws.

United Nations Relief and Rehabilitation Administration (UNRRA) An international relief agency created at a 44-nation conference in Washington, DC on November 9, 1943, to provide economic assistance and basic necessities to war refugees. It was especially active in repatriating and assisting refugees in the formerly Nazi-occupied European nations immediately after World War II.

USC Shoah Foundation Institute The foundation previously known as the Survivors of the Shoah Visual History Foundation, which was founded by American film director Steven Spielberg in 1994 as a result of his experience making the film *Schindler's List*. The foundation's mission is to record and preserve the testimonies of Holocaust survivors in a video archive and to promote Holocaust education. In 2006, after recording almost 50,000 international testimonies, the foundation became the USC Shoah Foundation Institute for Visual History and Education after partnering with the University of Southern California.

yarmulke (Yiddish; in Hebrew, *kippah*) A small head covering worn by Jewish men as a sign of reverence for God.

Zionism A movement promoted by the Viennese Jewish journalist Theodor Herzl, who argued in his 1896 book *Der Judenstaat* (The Jewish State) that the best way to resolve the problem of antisemitism and persecution of Jews in Europe was to create an independent Jewish state in the historic Jewish homeland of Biblical Israel. Zionists promoted the revival of Hebrew as a Jewish national language.

Photographs

1 Zuzana's mother, Vilma (née Stern) Weinberger. Humenné, Czechoslovakia, 1932.
2 Zuzana's father, Samuel Weinberger. Humenné, 1925.

Zuzana, age 3. Humenné, 1927.

1 Zuzana, age 10, in her Grade 4 class picture, sitting beside the teacher in the second row, fourth from the left. Of her twenty-four Jewish classmates, only four others survived. Humenné, 1934.

2 Zuzana, age 14, in her Grade 9 class picture, sitting in the second row, far right. Of her eight Jewish classmates, only one other survived. Humenné, 1938–1939.

1 Zuzana, age 12 (back row, centre), with her friends Irena (in front); Anna (far left) and Irma (far right). Humenné, 1936.

2 Zuzana, age 14 (right), with her friends Vera (centre) and Betty (left). Humenné,1938.

3 Zuzana, age 16 (right), wearing the mandatory yellow armband for Jews, with her friend Annie Moskovicova. Humenné,1940.

4 Zuzana (right) with her friends Regina (left) and Berta (centre), all wearing the now-mandatory yellow Star of David. Humenné, 1940.

1 Zuzana (back row, left) on a Hashomer Hatzair camping trip in 1940.

2 Zuzana with her friends Ernie (left) and Ladislav Grossman (right), who wrote the screenplay to the award-winning film *The Shop on Main Street* (1965). Humenné, 1940.

3 Zuzana and her friends in Humenné in 1941. From left to right: Jan, Bela, Viola, Zuzana, and Jan, whom she helped release from prison after the war.

1 Zuzana with her cousins in Humenné in 1939. In the back row, left to right, are
   Feri, Zuzana and Jozsi. Seated in front is Gyuri, a first cousin on her father's side,
   and Erwin.
2 Zuzana and Feri. Humenné, 1939.

1 Zuzana on her honeymoon in the High Tatras after the war. 1945.

2 Zuzana and Arthur Sermer in 1950.

3 Zuzana and Arthur with Victor (left) and a friend. Bratislava, 1947.

1 The Sermer brothers after the war. From left to right are Eman, Victor and
   Arthur. Bratislava, circa 1950.
2 The Sermer brothers and their wives in Toronto in the late 1970s. From left to
   right are Zuzana and Arthur, Eman and Yolana, and Victor and Mary.

1 Zuzana and Arthur Sermer with their grandchildren at their granddaughter Julie's bat mitzvah. Standing in the back row, left to right, are David, Mark, Tanya, Nicole and Julie. In the front row, left to right, are Corey, Arthur, Jessica, Zuzana and Becky. Toronto, 1996.

2 The whole Sermer family at Julie's bat mitzvah. Standing in the back row, left to right, are Zuzana's granddaughter Nicole; her son Mark; her daughter, Tamara; her son Paul; Paul's wife, Susan; her son Matthew's wife, Lillian; Matthew; her son Michael; Michael's wife, Margi; her granddaughter Tanya; and her granddaughter Julie. In the front row, left to right, are Zuzana's grandson David; Arthur Sermer; her grandchildren Corey and Jessica; Zuzana; and her granddaughter Becky. Toronto, 1996.

Zuzana's granddaughter Becky Sermer at her bat mitzvah. The Torah she is holding is the Czech Memorial Scroll originally from Uhlířské Janovice that was restored after the Holocaust by a philanthropic group in London, England. Connecticut, June 23, 2001.

1 Zuzana and Arthur at their son Michael's wedding. New York, 1983.
2 Zuzana and Arthur with their children at their daughter Tamara's wedding.
   Standing behind Zuzana and Arthur, left to right, are Michael, Tamara, Paul and
   Matthew. Toronto, 1996.

Zuzana and Arthur at their son Matthew's wedding. Toronto, 1990.

Index

The Azrieli Foundation was established in 1989 to realize and extend the philanthropic vision of David J. Azrieli, C.M., C.Q., M.Arch. The Foundation's mission is to support a wide spectrum of initiatives in education and research. The Azrieli Foundation is an active supporter of programs in the fields of Jewish education, the education of architects, scientific and medical research, and education in the arts. The Azrieli Foundation's many well-known initiatives include: the Holocaust Survivor Memoirs Program, which collects, preserves, publishes and distributes the written memoirs of survivors in Canada; the Azrieli Institute for Educational Empowerment, an innovative program successfully working to keep at-risk youth in school; and the Azrieli Fellows Program, which promotes academic excellence and leadership on the graduate level at Israeli universities.